MAXIMIZING EXAMINATION PERFORMANCE

A Psychological Approach

DON DAVIES

Kogan Page, London/Nichols Publishing, New York

Copyright © Don Davies 1986
All rights reserved

First published in Great Britain in 1986 by
Kogan Page Ltd, 120 Pentonville Road,
London N1 9JN

British Library Cataloguing in Publication Data
Davies, Don
 Maximizing examination performance: a
 psychological approach.
 1. Test anxiety   2. Examinations—
 Psychological aspects
 I. Title
 370.15   LB3060.6

 ISBN 1-85091-175-4

Published in the United States of America by
Nichols Publishing Company, Post Office Box 96,
New York, NY 10024

Library of Congress Cataloging-in-Publication Data

Davies, Don, 1926-
 Maximizing examination performance.

 Bibliography: p.
 1. Test anxiety. 2. Examinations—Psychological
aspects. 3. Universities and colleges—Examinations—
Psychological aspects. 4. Motivation in education.
I. Title.
LB3060.6.D38 1986   371.2'6   86-12495
ISBN 0-89397-254-1

Printed and bound in Great Britain by
Billing and Sons Ltd, Worcester

Contents

Introduction

A survey of the stress-related problems of 221 post-A level students[*] revealed that a substantial proportion (69 per cent) experienced stress-related problems both in the months preceding the examination and during the examination itself. These included poor concentration, persistent worries, panic reactions and certain minor health problems.

Examinations represent a measure of performance under stress. Public examinations commonly constitute one of the most extreme forms of competition in contemporary society. Examinations are stressful because they frequently exert pressures on people which call for much more than ordinary effort. Thus, they often become as much a measure of temperamental robustness and resilience as of knowledge and ability. Indeed, it is widely appreciated that the level of such emotional states as anxiety and excitability can make all the difference between passing and failing. None the less, for one reason or another, the whole emphasis on preparation for examinations invariably centres on the intellectual development of the individual and the acquisition of skill and knowledge. Systematic psychological preparation in the affective domain remains virtually nonexistent. The survey shows, for example, that only 7.7 per cent had received any form of training in the management of stress. A large proportion (40.1 per cent) indicated that they would have welcomed such help as part of their preparation.

It is evident that the greater the stress, the greater the need to succeed, the more important do emotional factors become in determining examination performance. High levels of anxiety generally tend to be associated with feelings of

[*] Davies, D. E. (1986) Examination performance: a survey of the stress-related problems of A level students. Unpublished survey.

insecurity, overcautiousness and indecision. In the tense atmosphere of the examination room the overanxious person can make simple errors which are quite untypical of his usual behaviour.

The ability of anxious people to concentrate is relatively poor and this is particularly so in conditions of stress. Anxious people tend to be self-critical, self-preoccupied and self-dissatisfied. Test situations evoke negative self-orientated responses which interfere with task concentration. In other words, the anxious person is often reacting to his own thoughts and emotions rather than to the demands of the examination situation. His attention tends to become more and more focused on his own internal thoughts and feelings. Poor concentration stems from two sources. These are a negative attitude or mood and the ease with which students are distracted from a set task. Anxious people tend to become worried about how poorly they are doing, how much better the others are and what people will think. The survey showed, for example, that 44 per cent of students were worried during the examination, and 11.2 per cent indicated that they worried in particular about other students being better. The negative attitude of high-anxious people is underlined by their tendency to ascribe failure to their lack of ability. In contrast, people of a more robust, stable disposition tend to believe that failure in their case can be put down to lack of effort. Thus, following failure stable people tend to respond with increased effort. The response of anxious people is to spend even more time worrying about their ability.

At high levels of anxiety performance is disrupted and behaviour is disorganized because the system is overactive. Some people become confused and, at the extreme, are reduced to a state of panic. Indications of such behaviour in test situations are seen when people switch to and fro from one question to another or when they respond with an 'everything except the kitchen sink' approach and simply fail to meet the specific demands of the question. In the survey 50.7 per cent reported experiencing panic reactions and 35.9 per cent panicked to the extent that they were switching to and fro from one question to another at various times during the examination. Despite much pre-examination advice there is an absence of planning and some students have for both worry and emotionality in addition to a test-anxiety score.

The accuracy of the above tests, as with all self-report measures, is generally influenced by such factors as honesty and the desire to create a favourable impression or to be seen in a 'good light'. Even when people try to be honest, however, the answers they give may not be objectively true. Neurotic people, for example, have a tendency to exaggerate their defects. They complain about aches and pains and about sleep problems to an objectively excessive degree. Generally, they tend to be more self-deprecative than people of a calmer and more stable disposition. Scores on self-report measures are also influenced by such factors as the personality of the tester, the time of day, experience of previous tests and temporary moodswings. In a review of self-report instruments to assess trait anxiety Tryon (1980) argues that the tests contain cues for participants who may be influenced in their replies by the demand characteristics of the situation. Tryon, in fact, concludes by saying that the tests are easily 'fakeable'. Clearly, the tests are inadequate by themselves except when used for research purposes with large groups of people. However, they can be useful as a guide and may be used in conjunction with other methods of assessment, such as interviews and systematic observation. Given on an individual basis in which 'good rapport' can be established, they serve as a useful 'lead in' to the problems of the test-anxious student and in this sense provide a valuable instrument for the tutor-counsellor.

Treatment of test anxiety

Treatment measures are discussed fully in the section on stress management in the following chapter. The terms stress management and test-anxiety reduction in the context of this book are used interchangeably. Treatment measures include relaxation, biofeedback training, systematic desensitization, cognitive modification, modelling behaviour, visualization and study skills training. It is open for people to employ those strategies which are most appropriate to their individual needs. Desensitization procedures, for example, have been shown to be particularly effective in the treatment of 'stage fright', which can occur in examinations involving a public performance of some kind.

Prevention is generally better than cure. It is helpful, therefore, to see that students are not exposed to acute failure experiences of examinations, the effects of which can be devastating in the case of the test-anxious student. Thus counselling services should really be made available well before examinations take place. The problem is that students can become *conditioned* to feeling anxious in situations to the detriment of performance.

Conclusion

Most test-anxious students have poor study habits and negative attitudes concerning their ability. Concentration under examination conditions tends to be poor. Early assessment and diagnosis of the condition is important. Treatment programmes need to be geared to the needs of individual students, the aim being that as a result of appropriate preparation in both the cognitive and affective domains the student will abe able to do reasonable justice to his ability and commitment. In situations of considerable stress, such as public examinations, the student is only likely to give of his best when he has been thoroughly prepared to meet the demands of the situation. Alex Main in his book *Encouraging Effective Learning* makes the point that much anxiety is avoidable if the student is adequately prepared. Most experienced people who have been trained to cope with pressure are able to adjust levels of activation to those which are commensurate with the task in hand. They are able, for example, to adjust arousal levels upwards or downwards as the demands of the situation change. In other words, they are in an appropriate state of readiness being neither over- nor under-aroused.

reported experiencing feelings of 'being rushed' when working in the presence of others.

From this it becomes evident that examinations effectively discriminate against the anxious individual. However, the general impression which seems to prevail is that examination stress is something which is virtually inevitable. Examinations are frequently viewed as being 'part and parcel' of school and college life and, therefore, students ought to be able to cope with the pressures or they should not be students at all.

Disputes in schools are likely to exacerbate the position for the overanxious student who likes a regular, well-established routine. Constant change and improvisation increase the uncertainty and heighten the pressures still further for the anxious student to the almost inevitable detriment of examination performance, for uncertainty is the harbinger of anxiety.

In the author's experience the help which is available for candidates with a stress problem is very limited, although this is through no lack of concern or a genuine desire to help on the part of others. But apart from resorting to pharmacological aids, help is generally limited to such advice as: 'Don't worry', 'Have a good night's rest', 'You'll be all right', 'Good luck!', 'Take some deep breaths', 'It'll soon be over', 'Take an aspirin', etc. It is very doubtful whether such advice is of much help. Indeed words of encouragement do nothing for the overanxious examinee in the same way as they do nothing for people with a fear of flying.

This book examines the motivational variables which are central to the development of ability and the acquisition of knowledge. Its major concern, however, is to examine those factors which generally operate in any stressful competitive situation, and to suggest guidelines for the maximization of examination performance. Apart from academic achievement the book has important implications for the emotional health of examination candidates and, indeed, for others facing situations perceived to be stressful.

Central to this particular area is work which assists a student to adjust emotionally to the rigorous demands of competitive examinations. The tutor's concern should be for the student himself as an individual. This is a concern which is generally well recognized as being of considerable importance and it receives due attention in the text. Because examinees differ in their personalities, attitudes and motivational drives, it follows that their psychic needs also differ. This means that they simply cannot all be treated in the same way.

Immediate pre-examination advice is likely to be of little value. Telling people to concentrate or to relax without telling them *how* is meaningless instruction. For candidates who are already overanxious, highly activated and excited, or to use the American expression 'psyched up', the so-called 'pep' talk is likely to be counterproductive and lead to a deterioration in performance. Indeed, with activation levels high above the optimum for maximum performance, it may be true to say that, in a very real sense, a candidate can, in fact, be trying too hard. As with the managers of some professional football clubs, exhorting highly aroused examinees to show still further effort is counterproductive, bringing some of them, like the players, to a state of near hysteria.

Psychological skills, such as confidence and concentration, are only acquired as a result of extensive practice. They cannot be gained overnight. Well-planned psychological preparation tailored to individual needs is required to assist candidates to perform at their peak or, to use the American jargon again, 'to come good on the day'. This book outlines a systematic approach to the ways in which the psychological skills of self-confidence and concentration can be developed, refined and sharpened to the extent that they become virtually automatic. In this book, a multifaceted approach is advanced which incorporates both cognitive and affective strategies, visualization or mental rehearsal, and the acquisition of positive attitudes by suggestion, autogenic techniques and the creation and completion of successful learning experiences. A relaxation programme is seen as an important feature of the total achievement strategy. The aim of the relaxation programme is for the state of relaxation to become a well-learned response; in this way the negative effects of anxiety are replaced by the positive benefits of relaxation which come in the form of greater confidence, improved concentration and increased efficiency arising from improved sleep and reduced fatigue.

This book has been written with the anxious examination candidate principally in mind. Performance in examinations is dependent to some extent on the ability to cope with the perceived stress of the situation. High levels of anxiety tend to be generally associated with feelings of insecurity, inadequacy and apprehension. Attitudes tend to be negative and there are often accompanying debilitating health effects.

In the survey 60.5 per cent of students felt that worry had an adverse effect on their health. As many as 33 per cent experienced sleeping difficulties and others were suffering from headaches and digestive problems up to six months before the examination. Not surprisingly, intellectual performance falls and in some instances is seriously disrupted. Anxious people invariably have little confidence in themselves. They have a 'thing' about examinations to the extent that in some cases the dominating concern in course selection becomes the method of assessment and not the subject! Systematic, prolonged, psychological preparation is seen as an essential requirement if the anxious examinee is to do reasonable justice to his ability and commitment.

It seems incredible that, some 80 years after Yerkes and Dodson first demonstrated with their dancing mice that high levels of anxiety disorganize behaviour and disrupt performance, students are not generally emotionally prepared for examinations. In an examination-orientated system this is an amazing omission in the secondary school curriculum, if not elsewhere. As it is, anxious candidates receive little help from their immediate associates simply because people do not know how to help. Thus, the majority of students are left to muddle through what is uncharted territory in a psychological sense. Readers who themselves have been anxious immediately before an examination, test, interview or public performance of some kind will probably agree that it can be a lonely time.

The implementation of systematic programmes tailored to individual needs in the affective domain would ensure a substantial reduction in the number of people who underachieve through unresolved emotional problems. And accordingly, absolute standards of achievement would show an appreciable improvement — as they are currently assessed.

The ability to perform well under pressure is a skill which can be learned. Strategies are advanced in this book for the management of stress and for the enhancement of performance in highly competitive situations.

The various motivational and emotional problems which

can beset students lend credence to the argument that just as an extended period is devoted to intellectual or academic preparation, so too should some time be spent in developing the emotional capacities of the overanxious student. The principal concern of psychological preparation is that the student should learn how to cope with stress situations to the extent that he is able to do reasonable justice to his ability and commitment. Psychological preparation is seen as incorporating a sustained systematic approach to an attainable standard of performance. The aim is to develop both the intellectual and emotional capacities of students to the extent that they have both the ability and confidence to deal with the many pressures which are an inherent feature of competitive examinations.

For our American readers, it should be explained that A level examinations are taken at the culmination of a student's school career at the age of 18 years. Performance at A level is graded on a five-point scale: A, B, C, D, E. Entry to universities, polytechnics and colleges of higher education is almost solely dependent upon a student's performance in the A level examinations. Passes in two or three subjects are generally required.

It should be noted that the male pronoun has been used throughout the book for stylistic reasons only. It covers both masculine and feminine genders.

Chapter 1

Motivation and Performance

Introduction

The study of motivation is important because it is almost
certainly the case that for various reasons many students fail
to fulfil their potential ability. The barrier to progress in
many areas of human performance is often a psychological
one — a classic example being the attempts to break the
four-minute mile in the early 1950s. The psychological
barrier is largely determined by a student's own expectations
of the standards he will reach. A number of principles and
strategies are advanced for motivating students to continue to
develop their abilities and skills. Because of the varying
psychological needs of particular students the importance of
an individual approach in teaching is emphasized. Thus, if a
teacher is to help to motivate a student he must really come
to know him as an individual.

Feedback, or knowledge of results, is basic to learning and
receives due attention in this chapter. Feedback not only
provides the learner with information concerning his performance but also serves as a reward, providing an extremely
strong incentive to continue a task since it relates to the
distance between a present state and a goal or objective. This
aspect of feedback is emphasized by many behavioural
theorists, notably Skinner (1953), who are concerned with
the role of rewards and punishments within the learning
situation.

The relationship between success, failure and motivation
is examined in relation to how this influences levels of
aspiration or expectancy of future success. The effect of
praise and criticism on the motivation of students is also
reviewed.

13

The teacher's expectation of a student's potential can be a very powerful factor influencing the motivation to continue to study. With respect to his examination performance a student will very often fulfil the expectations of his teacher, tending to do well if these are high and optimistic, and tending to do badly if they are low and pessimistic. There is, in fact, much research evidence in the education field concerning the powerful influence which the expectations of 'significant others' have on an individual's own motivation and expectations. By 'significant others' is meant the people who are perceived by the student as being important by virtue of their status, knowledge and expertise. In the school situation this is likely to be the teachers who are closely involved with the student, and at university or college the tutors. The expectations of parents can also have a strong influence on a student's performance.

Considerable attention is given to the relationship between the intensity of motivation, or level of arousal, and performance in competitive situations. Generally, people perform best at moderate levels of arousal and there is, in fact, an optimum level of arousal for maximum performance for each individual. It is at the two extremes of high and low levels of arousal that individuals do least well. Individual differences in levels of arousal or activation between students before competitive examinations mean that to perform at their best some students will need to be 'psyched up' and others to be 'psyched down', to use the American expressions. Care must be taken to see that students are not 'psyched out' by overconcerned, overanxious, and overambitious teachers and parents.

Ways in which motivation can be enhanced are discussed and the final section of this chapter is concerned with a very serious discussion of the relationships between the intensity of arousal and performance and the implications for the teacher or tutor, who can have a crucial role to play.

Motivation can be defined as being aroused to action, to directed, purposeful behaviour, although this may not necessarily be either efficient or effective. It is considered that there is a disturbance of equilibrium as the result of some organic or psychic need. The study of motivation is an important concern both with respect to the development of ability and the acquisition of skill and knowledge. It is also

14

equally important to have an understanding of why it is that individuals behave in situations at varying degrees of intensity. Pragmatically, a knowledge of motivation is important for two major concerns: the realization of the potential ability of the individual, and the maximization of his performance in the stressful competitive situation.

The term motivation denotes the factors and processes that impel people to action or inaction. Individuals are activated by many motives. There are the so-called primary needs such as food, drink and sleep, and then there are a considerable number of derived or learned motives including the desire for money, social status, security, and so forth.

Motives behind many actions, however, are often mixed and rather complicated. Woodworth (1921) has suggested that the organism possesses an inherent tendency 'to deal with its environment'. Similarly Stott (1966) considers that the driving force behind behaviour is a desire to operate effectively in one's surroundings. He suggests that some continuous process for maintaining effectiveness must be going on within the brain and that there is a continual checking for personal effectiveness.

Motivational levels tend to fall as the limits of ability are approached. This is partly due to the fact that there is a slowing down in the rate at which people are able to continue to improve. At moderate levels of ability progress can readily be seen and is sometimes quite marked. At the higher levels of performance, however, much of the time spent in study or practice will be spent solely in maintaining these levels. As people continue to improve this tends to be true to a progressively greater extent, with more and more time being spent simply in maintaining standards. Thus, at relatively high levels of performance it takes more effort and more time to improve further and it becomes increasingly difficult to make additional progress.

For many students the problem sooner or later becomes largely one of motivation. In many cases there is the belief that further improvement is simply not possible. If a student perceives that this is also the belief of his teacher then it is highly likely that these expectations of his limits will be confirmed. A teacher's expectation of performance is a powerful factor determining performance levels and has led to much research in the education field concerning the so-called self-fulfilling prophecy. Generally a person's performance tends to confirm the expectations of 'significant others' or those who are perceived as having some credibility. Thus, an optimistic approach by a tutor, teacher or coach tends to arouse higher motivational levels and expectations in the learner, and a pessimistic one tends to result in a lowering of those levels and expectations. The barrier to further progress is often a psychological one arising from a person's conviction that he cannot improve further. Once this psychological barrier can be overcome performance can continue to improve. A change in attitude, and above all in belief, is needed. In this the encouragement and positive approach of the teacher probably has a crucial role to play in nearly every case.

Intrinsic and extrinsic motivation

Motivation can take three main forms. These are intrinsic, extrinsic and a combination or interaction of these two. Extrinsic motivation refers to needs or motives which are largely external to the individual; that is to say, people are engaging in a particular activity or academic discipline for the rewards which go with success. They are principally motivated by financial returns, professional status or both. On the other hand, when a person is intrinsically motivated he is engaging in an activity for its own sake, for the satisfaction which this brings and, in the extreme, for the sheer enjoyment. Like Stott, Deci (1975) considers that intrinsically motivated behaviour is essentially a need for a person to feel competent and self-determining in dealing with his environment. Thus, the more people feel that their actions are self-determined and provide a sense of personal competence, the higher will be their level of intrinsic motivation. Deci's definition, with its emphasis on individual, internal feelings and perceptions, means that only the person in question can truly determine whether or not he is intrinsically motivated. It is apparent that many people find considerable satisfaction in having virtually complete mastery of a skill and being able to perform it in an expert fashion. They are not satisfied with moderate standards and go to great lengths to achieve perfection for the personal satisfaction which this brings. They enjoy the challenge of the pursuit of excellence. Intrinsic motivation is generally associated with

16

greater persistence and greater commitment. For people who are essentially extrinsically motivated to study, that is they are concerned mainly with the rewards which accompany achievement, if the rewards become difficult to achieve or unattainable they may well lose interest. The real danger also exists that where people are encouraged to study by being offered rewards they may sense that they are being manipulated, that other people are controlling their behaviour. The introduction of rewards can cause people to shift the location of their original perceived reason for performing the activity. Before being offered rewards people see their reasons as *inner* — a matter of their own free choice, but later people may see rewards as the *cause* of their activity. Thus, any classroom practice will decrease intrinsic motivation if it causes people to think that they are doing something for others. Therefore, it does happen that people who were initially intrinsically motivated lose this interest on being offered rewards and prizes. However, if the introduction of rewards heightens a person's feelings of competence, there will be an increase in intrinsic motivation. This happens if it results in the student seeing the achievement as being more valued and accordingly more prestigious. But in many instances students continue to study because they are both intrinsically and extrinsically motivated.

The following story illustrates how the introduction of rewards can cause a change from intrinsically to extrinsically motivated behaviour:

'An old man lived alone on a street where boys played noisily every afternoon. One day the din became too much, and he called the boys into his house. He told them he liked to listen to them play, but his hearing was failing and he could no longer hear their games. He asked them to come around each day and play noisily in front of his house. If they did, he would give them each a quarter. The youngsters raced back the following day and made a tremendous racket in front of the house. The old man paid them, and asked them to return the next day. Again they made noise, and again the old man paid them for it. But this time he gave each boy only 20 cents, explaining that he was running out of money. On the following day, they got only 15 cents each. Furthermore, the old man told them, he would have to reduce the fee to five cents on the fourth day. The boys became angry, and told the old man they would not be back. It was not worth the effort, they said, to make a noise for only five cents a day.'

(Casady, 1974)

17

Apart from controlling behaviour, as in the above story, rewards can also have an informational aspect. Rewards which provide information about progress can serve to enhance feelings of competence and self-determination and increase motivation. There are numerous instances of rewards which can operate in this way. Typical examples are examination grades, certificates and trophies of various kinds. All these provide the learner with information concerning his progress. However, if the controlling aspect of such rewards is seen to be salient the learner may lose interest, particularly if he sees his behaviour as being merely a means to an end.

With young people there exists the very real danger of this happening when they feel that they must excel to please their parents. It is well known that parents derive vicarious satisfaction from their children's accomplishments and some may exert considerable pressure upon them to succeed at all costs. Evidence for this can be seen in the thriving independent sector of school education, despite the crippling cost of this for those without a substantial income. All kinds of material rewards are offered to try to effect an increase in effort. The risk here is that the learner may lose intrinsic motivation for the activity because he may feel that he is being manipulated and controlled by such practices. Further, children may also become overanxious and overactivated to the detriment of learning and performance. What, in fact, is often generated is a very high level of unnecessary stress that can eventually undermine the confidence of even the temperamentally robust.

Finally, students who are intrinsically motivated are likely to be relatively well adjusted emotionally. Dorcus Butt in her book *The Psychology of Sport* argues that people who are competence-orientated are less likely to be upset by failure than people who are mainly motivated by external rewards such as financial incentives and social prestige. Butt argues that students who enjoy their subject, discipline or skilled activity, who are continually working towards perfection, are better able to withstand temporary setbacks. Following a reverse they can become principally concerned with analysing and evaluating their performance and the ways in which it can be improved. Attention is focused upon ability, knowledge and skill. Social considerations in this context are of secondary importance and the attendant stresses and anxieties are correspondingly less.

Contrary to popular belief, people often place great importance on being really good at a subject or skilled activity and not just on passing a test or examination. It is important, therefore, that situations are created which give the young person the opportunity to develop his ability, to pursue excellence. In the section which follows, strategies for enhancing the motivation of learners are outlined.

How to motivate students

A number of proven principles and strategies can be advanced for motivating individuals to continue to develop their abilities and refine their skills. However, the needs of learners vary so much that it is absolutely imperative that motivational strategies are individually focused. Differences in temperament, past experiences, attitudes and ability mean that for a teacher, tutor or coach to help a student he must get to know him as an individual. This can only be done by observing the student in a variety of situations over a period of time. Individual attention is particularly important because the same comments or criticisms can disturb one person considerably but leave another relatively unconcerned. Sensitive people, for example, may only be able to tolerate mild criticism while the tough-minded, extrovert student may benefit from having his weaknesses spelt out fairly emphatically.

It is of fundamental importance, therefore, that the tutor learns to recognize differences between individuals, not only with respect to intellectual maturity and ability but also in terms of emotional maturity and sensitivity if he is to motivate students successfully.

Motivational strategies

Many students need to be continually motivated. Outlined in this section are a number of proven strategies which will facilitate continuous motivation.

Planning objectives

First of all, it is important to plan goals or objectives. These need to be specific and realistic in that they should be attainable for the individual student. Goals should not be too easy, yet at the same time not too difficult, but should set a challenge. Thus goals set for individual students will vary according to their abilities and how much they can take in terms of challenge and difficulty. In facilitating the development of ability and the acquisition of knowledge, it is generally well recognized that students should participate in planning their objectives and which techniques and skills are to be developed and refined. In this way the student is made to feel more responsible and committed to the work in that he has some part to play in determining what he has to do. This is far more effective than telling people what they have to do. Discussion of goals, of the aims of study or practice sessions can be very valuable in providing the student with the opportunity to ask questions and to make suggestions. Thus, a concerted, mutually agreed approach means that a student is committed and becomes more personally involved. In this way students are likely to become more intrinsically motivated because they feel that their actions are self-determined and provide a sense of personal competence. They may see their contribution as being valued and giving them greater prestige, and in this way their commitment to any study programme is likely to be very substantially increased.

The setting up of mutually agreed objectives also means that the student is more closely concerned with the content of course programmes. Need achievement theory (McClelland 1953) suggests that students ought to be aware of the point or the rationale of particular methods of study and practice drills. The author has observed lessons where the students were listless and poorly motivated simply because they were 'in the dark' concerning the relevance of the activities for the development of skill and the improvement of performance.

The overriding consideration in any learning situation is to have a happy and secure emotional 'climate' created through satisfying, consistent, harmonious relationships and interesting, meaningful projects. The idea is that students will simply want to learn more and more about the subject for the sheer satisfaction which this brings. In this way study or practice is not merely seen as a means to an end, such as the passing of an examination or the obtaining of a qualification. Competence-orientated people gain considerable satisfaction from the activity itself and are accordingly highly motivated.

Television provides an opportunity to observe at close range people who are quite obviously dominantly competence-orientated. Performers who spring readily to mind are the Golfers Jack Nicklaus and Sevvy Ballesteros and, in music, Yehudi Menuhin. These are people who strive for the perfection of their art. Of course, the jaundiced, sceptical reader might consider that these are the same people who the next day will go 'smiling all the way to the bank'.

Knowledge of results or feedback

Knowledge of the results of performance, or feedback, is basic to learning. Bilodeau and Bilodeau (1961) concluded that studies of feedback and knowledge of results show it to be 'the strongest, most important variable controlling performance and learning'.

Classical studies by Thorndike (1927) and by Trowbridge and Cason (1932) serve to underline the importance of knowledge of results in terms of the information value. In the course of acquiring skill it is important for the learner to realize the connection between his action and the result.

Research by Elwell and Grindley (1938) stressed the motivational aspect of feedback which, apart from providing information concerning performance, also serves as reward providing an extremely strong incentive to continue a task, since it relates to the distance between a present state and a goal. This aspect of feedback is emphasized by many behavioural theorists, notably Skinner (1953), who are concerned with the role of rewards and punishments within the learning situation.

Welford (1968) stressed the importance of the specificity of the information which the learners receives. Thus, the use of precise aids, such as graphs and tables, provides the learner not just with knowledge, but also act as important motivational devices since the learner gets some idea of standards and is able to see with some clarity not only his own progress and attainment but also the difference between his own and the performance levels of students of a higher standard.

Precise, objective information concerning the quality of his work means that a student is able to see for himself how his current performance differs from his previous results. He is able to monitor and assess his performance in the light of variations in study methods and technique, and additionally

21

his learning is continually being reinforced. Therefore, precise knowledge of results is a powerful motivating force for the student in maintaining study over long and arduous periods in preparation for an important, demanding examination.

People concerned with a student's progress may sometimes say that he is doing well in order to boost his morale. Such remarks may be imprecise and will be of little help to the student who is in doubt concerning the accuracy of such comments. Thus, the value for the student of objective knowledge of progress in terms of grades, marks, corrected scripts, etc cannot be overestimated. It seems likely, for example, that a student with confirmed knowledge of his developing ability is likely to become more confident and it is almost certain that he will perceive particular situations as being less stressful than formerly because of his greater ability.

Reinforcement

Any behaviour or action which is followed by pleasing consequences tends to increase the probability of that behaviour or action occurring again; likewise, any behaviour or action culminating in unpleasant consequences tends to decrease the probability of that behaviour occurring again. Pleasing consequences which follow any action mean that behaviour is being positively reinforced. Positive reinforcement can come in various forms. It can come in the form of self-knowledge or awareness in so far as the student is able to relate what he does to the results. He may, for example, associate a high grade with a particular method of preparation. Positive reinforcement can also come in the form of the tutor praising or acknowledging a good performance at the time it is made. Appreciation of a particular performance by other students can also be a strong positive reinforcer increasing the probability of the student being able to repeat such a performance in the future.

In helping a person to improve, the principles of reinforcement need to be applied systematically to be effective. The first step is to determine the factors which are important for maximizing skilled performance. As was stated earlier, goals or objectives need to be well defined and as specific as possible. In this way a student has something concrete or definite towards which to direct his energies. Additionally, where goals are specified, progress can be evaluated and the information can be used to restructure any study or skill development programme. Any advance which the student makes towards acquiring a new or improved skill should be immediately reinforced and delivered emphatically to indicate its importance. Reinforcement also needs to be both clear and specific. The idea is to start with heavy almost constant reinforcement and then to gradually reduce it so that reinforcement is only being given intermittently. In the later stages of learning, reinforcement should be somewhat infrequent otherwise it will lose its value. Students who are improving are also being supported by internal reinforcers which emanate from increasing satisfaction and a pride in achievement.

The tutor can reinforce a student's improving performance and developing ability in several ways. He can praise performance verbally by saying 'good', 'well done' or 'that's much better'. Alternatively, he might nod or clap, raise his arms, give a thumbs up sign, etc. In the perceptual-motor domain the coach can also provide reinforcement by setting up targets or by measuring the speed of certain strokes, such as the service in tennis.

Success and failure

It is important to arrange successful experiences for learners. Situations in which students consistently fail must be avoided. An early history of failure in a subject invariably means that students become poorly motivated and lose interest. This is almost certain to be the case if failure is followed by criticism from teachers and parents. Successful experiences lead to an increase in the level of aspiration. That is to say that with success individuals begin to raise their sights and expect to do better than before. Failure, on the other hand, generally leads to a decrease in aspiration levels. The important consideration here is that the level of aspiration or of expectancy of success is very closely related to the level of performance or of actual success. Invariably, it is the case that if people expect to succeed then they do so, if they expect to fail then they fail. In the early stages of learning a subject or of acquiring a skill, students should experience considerable success in competitive or stressful situations. Young people are encouraged to continue by success and the study programme should be so designed that individuals, in their own view, have more successes than failures. Successes and failures do not necessarily equate with high marks and low marks; it is really a matter of degree. A student, for example, could well see a 'fail' as a 'success' if he attained a mark which was above his expectations in a difficult examination. At the same time a pass in a test of low standing might hardly count as a success and could well be ignored.

For the experienced student who has already made some progress, the best results seem to come from a mixture of failure and success. The danger with a long period of continued success is that this can lead to boredom, disinterest and complacency. Studying the subject no longer presents much of a challenge and there is little excitement for the student. Certainly, it seems to be the case that the occasional failure can act as an incentive to try harder and in this way can be highly motivating.

People with a long history of chronic failure invariably become poorly motivated with correspondingly low levels of aspiration. There is a strong tendency to abandon the activity in search of success elsewhere. However, with appropriate strategies it is possible to raise aspiration levels, even in the case of the student who has become despondent and pessimistic. In this situation a series of small, progressive goals should be set which result in a series of repetitive successes. A number of intermediate goals should be set which span the distance between the individual's initial level of attainment and the final level of attainment which is desired. Repeated success experiences should lead to raised aspiration levels which, in turn, should influence further progress. Arranging successful experiences for the learner is an effective motivating strategy. However, it is important to use the strategy correctly and to consider such factors as age, ability, the individual's perception of the difficulty of the task and the extent to which his attitudes have been influenced by past experience. Generally, people will be poorly motivated if they see an assignment as being either too easy or too difficult. Additionally, the importance of the situation influences arousal levels and intensity of behaviour. This latter issue is discussed at length in the final section of this chapter and is referred to again at various other stages of the book.

Praise and criticism

It is difficult to generalize about the effect upon students of the use of praise and criticism by the teacher. People vary markedly in their reactions to praise and criticism because of personality differences and the degree to which they perceive themselves to be succeeding in the activity or subject. The effect of any praise, criticism or advice will also be determined by a student's opinion of his teacher, tutor or coach. People who are held in high esteem by the learner will have a much greater influence than those who are held in relatively low esteem and are seen as having little credibility. Here, it is the individual student's own perception which is the important factor. Generally, however, praise which the student perceives as warranted is a powerful incentive to continue to study or practise.

It seems to be the case that students who are doing relatively well in a subject are helped by being given justifiable, constructive criticism which is concerned with specific technical suggestions for improvement. It is the specific technical advice which is most appreciated by students. Exhortations to be positive, to concentrate, or try harder are of little avail because in the absence of being instructed how to do these things the terms are meaningless to students.

Too much praise, especially if it is unwarranted, is likely to have little effect and can be counterproductive, leading to a decrease in motivation. It can also be irritating, for example, in the case of an intelligent student who clearly sees that he is not improving. Praise must be deserved and must be seen to be so. It should, of course, be given immediately and can be given for effort, for results or for both. There is also the risk that the overuse of praise might result in individuals becoming extrinsically- rather than intrinsically-orientated, and becoming more interested in the symbolic reward of praise than the activity itself.

Thus, the use of a mixture of praise and criticism seems to be the best tactic for students who are making progress in a subject or skilled activity. However, because students vary so widely in their reactions to advice, it is imperative that the teacher approaches each student in terms of his sensitivity and his past and current performance in tests and examinations. Sensitive, withdrawn students tend to be adversely affected by a negative critical approach while the confident, successful student will generally benefit from having his errors pointed out — even quite emphatically. Thus, the same comments, the same approach, can emotionally disturb some students but leave others unaffected. There is considerable evidence to the effect that a combination of praise and criticism tends to be better than praise or criticism used alone.

Individual teaching and recognition

Several references are made throughout this book to the importance of an individual approach to teaching. Students need to have regular individual attention and be made to feel that they have some special contribution to make towards the work of the group. This gives the student a sense of belonging, of affiliation, and gives him a feeling of ease and security. His motivation thereby is enhanced. Students also need to feel that their accomplishments, even in activities away from school or college, are being noticed; the teacher should establish contact with the student to show his interest. Such recognition must come fairly close in time to the event or it will lose much of its significance in terms of enhancing motivation.

The importance of taking an individual interest in people was demonstrated in a series of experiments carried out by the Western Electric Company at their plant in Chicago, USA from 1926 to 1939. Various changes were made to the working conditions at the site. These included better lighting and heating, and improved rest and refreshment periods: production rose. However, manipulating the changes in various ways, whether for better or worse, did not affect production. Extensive investigation failed to identify any particular tangible factor which was resulting in increased output. The management was eventually forced to the conclusion that production was improving not because of any single improvement in the working conditions, but because the workforce had felt that a special interest was being taken in them as people. This special interest resulted in a general improvement in morale and increased endeavour. This extremely interesting and valuable investigation initiated a considerable amount of research into the importance of the study of individual differences for motivation and learning. As a result it is now well established that, while certain motivational techniques and approaches may benefit some people, they have an adverse effect upon others. For performance in stressful competitive situations, for example, some people need to be calmed down while others have to be urged to show greater commitment and effort.

Competition

Competition during study and practice sessions can be an incentive and a useful motivational technique provided it is used wisely and is closely related to the needs of individuals. Moderate competition between students provides interest and enjoyment, but it can be disastrous and destroy morale if too much importance is attached to the results. Motivation will also be weakened if an individual is either being continually outclassed or is surpassing the other students with ease. Competition between low-skilled people tends to disrupt performance but for highly skilled people performance tends to be enhanced.

An excellent motivational strategy is for a student to compete against himself; that is, he competes against his own previous level of performance, score, mark or standard. Competition against the self presents a meaningful challenge and it also avoids undue stress and social friction which can occur when students compete against each other. A student can also compete and measure his performance against particular standards which have been established by students in the past. Competing against the self means that situations must be created which provide the student with objective knowledge of the results of his performance. In this respect, graphs and charts of progress for the personal attention of the student are a useful motivating device.

Finally, it seems to be the case that the learner persists in studying and practising if he has publicly stated his intentions or goals. The prospect that his associates will be making periodic enquiries concerning his progress seems to act as an incentive for the learner to continue to work towards his stated goals. The commitment to the task is increased and this may be because the individual, in a situation of his own creation, has become more accountable for his actions.

Motivation and performance

Motivation has been discussed so far with regard to developing ability and acquiring knowledge in terms of commitment, study and practice. The following section is concerned with the intensity of motivation in terms of arousal, or of activation of the nervous system and how this influences performance in a competitive examination context. Some psychological aspects of intellectual performance are discussed at length and in some depth. Guidelines are outlined which help students to be at their best emotionally for an examination. Because of the widely differing needs of individual students, the importance of an individual approach is underlined; students cannot all be helped in the same way. Some may be 'psyched up', for example, to the extent that they fail to do justice to their abilities in a competitive examination. Temperament, ability and past examination experiences are important factors to take into account in planning the appropriate motivational strategy.

Earlier in this chapter reference was made to the study of the intensity of motivation and how motives actually operate rather than what they are. The intensity of motivation is a crucial factor in performance in competitive situations and the rest of this chapter is given over to a discussion of arousal levels and how these operate either to improve, depress or even severely inhibit performance. Research in this area, therefore, is concerned with levels of arousal in the organism and indicates the intensity of behaviour. Arousal refers to the degree of activation of the nervous system. The level of arousal can be regarded as a continuum of activity ranging from deep sleep at one end, through medium levels and on to a high degree of intense concentration at the other. Physiological methods exist to measure arousal levels, although a major problem here is that physiological reactions tend to be highly individualistic and need to be supported by other measures of assessment.

The skin presents a certain resistance to the passage of an electric current and when an individual becomes emotionally aroused this resistance is lowered as a result of an increase in perspiration. Conductance levels are high when the individual is alert, interested or anxious and they fall as an individual becomes sleepy, bored or well adjusted to situations. Indices commonly used to measure levels of arousal are skin conductance and the galvanic skin response.

Conductance indicates an individual's habitual position on

a continuum from low to high activation. The galvanic skin response, on the other hand, reflects more an individual's temporary state of activation or tension. Other measures of autonomic activity include heart and pulse rate, respiration and electrocortical activity. The responses vary with each specific situation as well as with those organic factors which are peculiar to each individual. However, although these individual differences exist, it is clear that the entire person becomes activated and responds to increasing arousal levels. Personality differences have been found to exist with extroverts having an habitually lower level of arousal than introverts (Claridge and Herrington, 1960) and with neurotic individuals being more readily aroused in stressful situations than stable people (Davies et al., 1963). However, not only are there differences between individuals regarding activation levels, but these also vary for the same person according to the time of day (Blake, 1967). In this respect Colquhoun and Corcoran (1964) also found the performance of introverts, in relation to that of extroverts, to be superior in the morning but that extroverts did better in the evening.

What has emerged from research is that the relationship between arousal level, as measured by skin conductance and performance of difficult tasks, is not a linear one. Generally, performance tends to increase with higher levels of arousal up to an optimum following which, at extreme levels, performance declines (Duffy, 1957; Stennett, 1957). Welford (1968) has suggested that performance improves as arousal level increases from its low level because impulses from the brain often render the cortex more sensitive and responsive. What is less clear, he says, is why performance should decline at very high levels of arousal. Welford considers that the simplest explanation is that with an intense stream of impulses from the brain stem the cells in the cortex actually fire. As a result of this, outside signals would be blurred and cells normally used for carrying messages would be refractory and the capacity of the brain accordingly lowered. This view could help to explain why high levels of arousal inhibit performance of more difficult and complex tasks, though performance of relatively simple tasks is unaffected, and indeed can be facilitated, by high activation. However, the relationship between arousal and performance is generally not so simple or clear-cut as it is depicted in Figure 1.

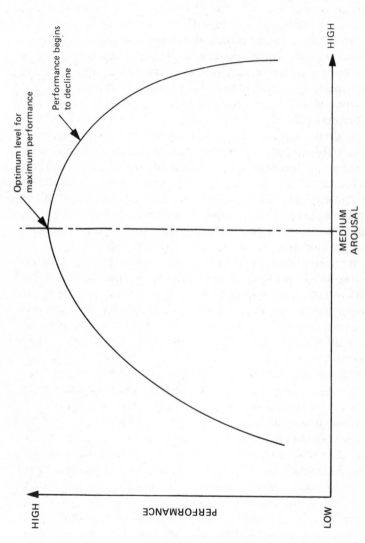

Figure 1 *Arousal levels and performance*

A number of mediating factors operate to influence the nature of this relationship and serve to make it rather more complex. These include personality, ability, the need for achievement and an individual's past experience of similar situations, among others. They are examined in detail at later stages of the book.

The introduction of stress to a learning situation in the form of a more difficult task or of various incentives involves activation of the autonomic nervous system with an increase in the level of arousal. Thus, mild stress could well be associated with an improvement of performance and severe stress with a deterioration of performance due to individuals becoming over-aroused. Occasionally individuals panic under severe stress and there is a breakdown in learning and a return to a more primitive or earlier form of response. The intensity of motivation would appear to be an essential feature of the operation of the feedback mechanism that underlies skilled performance. Action is initiated by signals which arise when departure from the optimum occurs. As departure from the optimum becomes greater, so the signals and the resulting action increase in intensity, if necessary to the point at which the limit of the capacity of the mechanism is reached. On the other hand, the intensity of the action becomes less powerful as departure from the optimum decreases.

Two examples may suffice to illustrate this theory, the first of which stems from an alarming incident experienced by the author off the southern coast of Spain in 1974. In the first example a person swimming in the sea, suddenly finding himself some distance from the shore, decides he is too far out and decides to swim back. His actions become increasingly vigorous as he finds himself being carried further out to sea; on the other hand, his actions diminish in intensity as he approaches the shore and the security of more shallow water. Example two concerns a student taking an examination who begins to run out of time. As the remaining time decreases relative to the amount of work to be completed, his actions are speeded up until, with only a few minutes left, the student becomes engaged in a frenzy of activity virtually amounting to panic; in some instances, there is a disintegration of rational behaviour. In the author's survey, for example, 50.7 per cent of examination students experienced panic reactions which included switching to and fro from one question to another.

The effectiveness of such a system, and the rewarding and punishing effects of actions, obviously depend on the feedback loop from output to input being closed; that is, upon the subject having effective knowledge of the results of his actions. In optimal conditions of stress such knowledge not only enables a person to adjust his behaviour and to correct errors, but also has an activating and incentive effect.

It is possible to elaborate from this simple feedback model to account for a number of situations in which behaviour becomes more or less intense and accounts for wide variations in individual performance. Under the stress of competition some people underachieve, some overachieve and some confirm and live up to expectations. People who do far worse under examination conditions than in practice are frequently unable to cope emotionally and to control arousal levels. Overachievers, on the other hand, tend to find coursework situations somewhat boring and need the stress which is presented by an examination to become optimally aroused. Generally speaking, those people who do no better and no worse under competitive conditions are people with low achievement needs. They are, therefore, unaffected by a competitive situation because they perceive it as being no more stressful than everyday conditions.

An example of an underachiever is a deputy headmistress who was taking her first degree examinations almost in middle-age. She was able and committed, but in a three-hour examination managed to write little more than a dozen or so words. This is an example of an individual 'freezing' and being unable to perform. Another form of panic behaviour can be observed in highly motivated people who write a great deal in examinations, but not to the point. As a university examiner for over ten years, the author read a number of lengthy scripts which had clearly been written in great haste. The impression they gave was that the writers were putting down everything they knew about the topic and more besides. They were, however, generally lacking in any coherent analysis of the problem or issue posed by the question.

Since activation or arousal levels have been seen to be directly related to performance, there are important implications with respect to preparation for examinations.

Conditions have to be arranged which will produce a more or less optimum level of arousal if people are to do justice to their ability and commitment. This is a difficult task, as people differ both behaviourally and physiologically in their reactions to competitive situations and the way in which stress is perceived. Thus some individuals are generally tense, others are tense only in certain muscle groups. Heart rates also vary among people under stress, as does palm sweating. The position is exacerbated by the fact that a highly stressful situation for one person is not necessarily so for another. However, in general it has been found that for most competitive activities an arousal level rather above the normal is the optimum, but this should not be too high. The question of optimizing arousal levels for maximum performance is discussed later in the book. Clearly a comprehensive and accurate assessment of the needs of individual people is a necessary prerequisite in the design of programmes aimed at optimizing arousal levels.

Optimum arousal levels vary according to the nature of the activity. Oxendine (1970) considers that with the paucity of evidence available in the sports field it is only possible to be speculative about optimum levels of activation for particular sports activities. He argues that relatively high levels of activation will be optimal for activities which are not complex, which do not require fine muscle control and where the emphasis is on speed and strength. This would be consistent with the findings of Lowe (1971) which showed that high levels of activation facilitated the performance of easy tasks. On the other hand, Oxendine believes that with complex tasks, and where the emphasis is on fine muscle control, maximum performance is likely to be associated with relatively lower levels of arousal. Thus, according to this view, high levels of arousal would be beneficial for sprinters but not for golfers when it comes to putting. The benefits of speed, Oxendine argues, would be maximized for the sprinter whereas excessive muscular tension would adversely affect the fine muscle control required to putt successfully.

Martens (1974) advances the view that for each athletic activity a range of activation levels might be the optimum for maximum performance. He further considers that the extent of any range will vary according to the nature of the activity. Like Oxendine, he considers that the main dimensions of a task determining optimum activation levels are the complexity and the amount of energy involved. Martens quotes Fiske and Maddi (1961) as postulating that the range of optimum arousal will decrease as tasks become more difficult. Martens also considers that the optimum range of arousal is likely to contract still further for complex activities which also demand more energy. According to these postulates optimum arousal levels in such sports as tennis and fencing will not only be relatively difficult to achieve but also to maintain.

Away from the stress of competition, optimizing activation levels in practice sessions is more straightforward. Here the intensity of motivation of individuals will be strongly influenced by the goals or objectives which are established. These must be meaningful and it helps if people are allowed to co-operate in their planning. Activation is likely to be optimal when the objectives are just within reach of a student's ability and, therefore, present a stimulating challenge. On the other hand, with goals which are too easy a student is likely to become bored and disinterested, and with goals which are too difficult will tend to become despondent and eventually give up.

This discussion has centred upon factors likely to influence activation levels. These include the perceived difficulty of the task, the type of activity, the personality of the individual, the degree of incentive present and an individual's past experience of similar situations. Additionally, such factors as physical and emotional health, and the differential effects of particular social contexts such as audience effects (Cox, 1966) further complicate the issue. The importance, and the way in which these several factors interact seem likely to vary from one situation to another, and it would require a major clinical study to assess their relationships to activation levels even for one event.

With present knowledge it is possible to set out broad, general guidelines for teachers, tutors and coaches, and to underline the importance of the affective dimensions influencing learning and performance and the emotional needs of the individual in the competitive situation.

Although it may prove difficult to manipulate conditions in order to optimize arousal levels, it should at least be possible to avoid the pitfalls which engender underactivation or overactivation in the student.

Competitive situations, whether in education or elsewhere, are frequently riddled with exhortations for people to make more effort and to try much harder. However, where arousal levels are far above the optimum for maximum performance, it may be true to say that a person is, in fact, trying too hard.

References

Bilodeau, E. A., and Bilodeau, I. McD. (1961) Motor skills learning. *The Annual Review of Psychology.* 12, 243-80.

Blake, M. J. F. (1967) The relationship between circadian rhythm of body temperature and introversion-extroversion. *Nature.* 215, 896-7.

Butt, D. S. (1976) *The Psychology of Sport: The Behaviour, Motivation, Personality and Performance of Athletes.* Van Norstrand Reinhold, New York.

Casady, M. (1974) The tricky business of giving rewards. *Psychology Today.* 8 (4), 52.

Claridge, G. S. and Herrington, R. N. (1960) Sedation threshold, personality and the theory of neurosis. *Journal of Mental Science.* 106, 1568-83.

Colquhoun, W. P. and Corcoran, D. W. J. (1964) The effects of time of day and social isolation on the relationship between temperament and performance. *British Journal of Social and Clinical Psychology.* 3, 226-31.

Cox, F. N. (1966) Some effects of test anxiety and presence or absence of other persons on boys' performance on a repetitive motor task. *Journal of Experimental Child Psychology.* 3, 100-12.

Davies, D. E. (1980) The potential tennis champion. *School Sport.* 5, (1), 21.

Davies et al. (1963) Sedation threshold, autonomic ability, and the excitation-inhibition theory of personality. The blood pressure response to an adrenaline antagonist as a measure of autonomic ability. *British Journal of Psychoanalysis.* 109, 558-67.

Deci, E. L. (1975) *Intrinsic Motivation.* Plenum, New York.

Duffy (1957) The psychological significance of the concept of 'arousal' or 'activation'. *Psychology Review.* 64, 265-75.

Elwell, J. L. and Grindley, G. C. (1938) Effects of knowledge of results on learning and performance. *British Journal of Psychology.* 29, 39-54.

Fiske, D. W. and Maddi, S. R. (eds) (1961) *Functions of varied experience.* Homewood. 1, 11. Dorsey.

Lowe, R. (1971) Stress, arousal and task performances of little league basketball players. Unpublished PhD thesis, University of Illinois.

McClelland, D. C., et al. (1953) *Achievement Motivation.* Appleton-Century-Crofts, New York.

Martens, R. (1974) Arousal and motor performance. In J. H. Wilmore (ed.) *Exercise and Sport Science Reviews.* 2, 155-88.

Oxendine, J. B. (1970) Emotional arousal and motor performance. *Quest*. xiii, 18-22.

Skinner, B. F. (1953) *Science and Human Behaviour*. Macmillan, New York.

Stennett (1957) The relationship of performance level to level of arousal. *Journal of Experimental Psychology*. 54, 54-61.

Stott, D. H. (1966) *Studies of Troublesome Children*. Tavistock, London.

Thorndike, E. L. (1927) The law of effect. *American Journal of Psychology*. 39, 212-22.

Trowbridge, M. A., and Cason, H. (1932) An experimental study of Thorndike's theory of learning. *Journal of General Psychology*. 7, 245-60.

Welford, A. T. (1968) *Fundamentals of Skill*. Methuen, London.

Woodworth, R. S. (1921) *Psychology*. Methuen, London.

Chapter 2

Anxiety and Performance

Anxiety is a diffuse, affective condition which can be mal-adaptive in its functions. The problem concerning anxiety is often its vagueness. We cannot always explain why we feel as we do, what it is we are anxious about or what we fear may happen. People report that they just feel anxious and that they cannot rid themselves of very uncomfortable, unpleasant feelings. They feel that way almost as though they are caught in some kind of emotional trap from which they are powerless to escape. Anxiety can be chronic, like dull toothache, and can be debilitating, extending over long periods of time and affecting things like sleep and appetite. Anxiety can also be acute and experiences can be intensely painful with people becoming jumpy and irritable.

Trait and state anxiety

Anxiety is regarded both as a trait or personality factor and also as a state or situational factor. Trait anxiety is the relatively enduring disposition to psychological stress or the extent to which an individual is fearful in most situations. State anxiety, on the other hand, refers to the degree of anxiety an individual feels when confronted with a specific stressful situation. It is the individual's transitory and sub-jective reaction to a consciously perceived threat regardless of the actual danger. Interactions have been found to exist between the two variables of trait and state anxiety. People with a high level of trait anxiety report greater intensities of state anxiety in threatening situations more frequently than people with a low level of trait anxiety. The person with a high trait or chronic anxiety will respond to more situations with a high degree of state anxiety than will the low trait-anxiety person. That is not to say that a low trait-anxiety person will never show a high level of state anxiety; it is important to understand that the number of situations which result in a high level of state anxiety are much greater for the high trait-anxiety person (Sarason, 1960). Consequently, in the examination situation the high trait-anxious person is more likely to experience a high state anxiety. State anxiety is very much dependent on the individual's cognitive interpretations of situations or the way in which they are appraised.

The distinction between anxiety viewed as a personality trait and anxiety viewed as a temporary situational state can be seen by looking at the form of a particular instrument or test designed to measure anxiety levels. The State-Trait-Anxiety Inventory (STAI) of Spielburger et al. (1970) measures both trait and state anxiety by two separate sub-scales each consisting of 20 items or statements. With respect to state anxiety, the person's response gives a subjective indication of the degree of intensity of his feeling at that moment. Thus on a four-point scale to the statement 'I'm calm' the alternatives are as follows:

1. not at all,
2. somewhat,
3. moderately so,
4. very much so.

With respect to trait anxiety the items consist of statements of the type 'I feel pleasant', 'I lack self-confidence', and 'I worry too much over something that doesn't matter'. The respondent is asked, again on a four-point scale, to estimate how *often he usually feels this way:*

1. almost never,
2. sometimes,
3. often,
4. almost always.

Each of the assessments on the trait scale, therefore, is relatively stable over time and is not subject to situational stress factors.

Causes of anxiety

It was Sigmund Freud who stressed the anticipatory nature of anxiety; we are anxious lest something should occur. Thus, examination candidates expect to succeed at some examinations and to fail at others. Even before the examination begins, therefore, they become more or less anxious according to whether they expect to succeed or fail. More able people are likely to be less adversely affected by the inhibiting effects of high anxiety than less able people because they perceive examinations as being relatively less difficult. For example, it is likely that an individual would experience variations in state anxiety levels when performing the following activities under competitive conditions:

1. Making a speech.
2. Taking an examination in statistics.
3. Playing a musical instrument.
4. Climbing a rock face.

Thus, the level of skill of an individual could be an important mediating factor between anxiety state and performance (Fenz and Epstein, 1969).

An individual who interprets or perceives a situation as being threatening to his status and self-esteem is likely to experience an increase in anxiety accompanied by an elevation of physiological measures of arousal, ie heart rate, blood pressure. The fear of failure is a potent cause of anxiety and it follows that the more keen a person is to succeed the more anxious he is likely to become and the more seriously failure will be taken. The level of state anxiety a person exhibits is not only related to trait anxiety but also to certain situational variables. One of these, as has been seen, is the importance of the event for the individual and another is the uncertainty of the outcome. Previous experience of similar situations is also an important variable and people become anxious not to repeat humiliating situations which have arisen from failure. For the anxious student the position is likely to be exacerbated if parents or teachers themselves are overanxious and overconcerned. Anxiety readily transmits from person to person and young people, when parents or teachers are overanxious, will be quickly aware of this.

Fathers and mothers can, of course, be far too ambitious for their children; by attaching too much importance to academic achievement the anxiety and stress for the student are increased. The social pressures which are generated are sometimes so great that it is not unknown for people to be physically sick before an examination. Heightened anxiety levels, as will be seen later in this chapter, can be detrimental to performance.

High levels of anxiety tend to be generally associated with feelings of insecurity, overcautiousness and indecision. There is almost inevitably a feeling of inadequacy and a loss of confidence. Thus in competitive examinations, overanxious students are likely to be hesitant and to have difficulty in adapting to new situations which are strange and unfamiliar, such as a different building or room, an invigilator who is a stranger and the presence of a large number of other candidates. The behaviour of the highly anxious person tends to be rigid, inflexible, stereotyped and, therefore, predictable. The highly anxious person is slower to react in the stressful competitive situation than he is in the relatively relaxed conditions of practice. At tense, crucial moments during a test or interview, for example, the overanxious individual can be seized with self-doubt, panic and may become 'tongue-tied'. Anxiety affects candidates in different ways; some become tense and rigid, others become very active but in an ineffective way. Nearly all become overconcerned with their own performance. Furthermore, they tend to be easily distracted by stimuli which should be irrelevant, such as the presence of other people, the temperature of the room, any minor outside noise, etc. Concentration sometimes becomes so poor that candidates fail to notice important conditions and alternatives set out in the paper, such as the number of questions and the choices available. From this it becomes clear that a high level of anxiety disrupts and disorganizes behaviour through a lowering of attention, concentration and intellectual control.

Mechanisms of ego defence

A high level of anxiety is frequently accompanied by unpleasant, discomforting emotional feelings and also by various painful psychosomatic symptoms, such as headaches, stomach cramps and vomiting. Because of such discomfort highly anxious people are strongly motivated to find a means of escape. They frequently do so by resorting to various mechanisms of ego defence.

Defence mechanisms are frequently employed as a means by which people preserve their self-concept. Defence mechanisms are learned responses to situations. They appear to develop almost unconsciously in people and in some instances are undesirable, since they do not represent a positive approach either to evaluating or solving a problem. The problem often remains. Everyone uses these mechanisms to some extent and daily examples of their uses are to be found in both school and college. Defences which people commonly adopt are self-deceptive, and the type of defence chosen depends on the causal nature of the anxiety, the personality of the individual and his own previous experiences of a specific situation, such as an examination or interview for example. When a defence is used some aspect of reality is usually distorted and people will often exaggerate or even imagine their own feelings and perceptions.

Defence mechanisms are generally not particularly effective. Sometimes they are employed as a temporary measure to deal with situations and sometimes they may be used on a long-term basis. To a certain extent the use of defence mechanisms is normal behaviour and most people adopt some of them at one time or another. Indeed, when under undue pressure the use of a defence can be healthy self-protection. It is when these mechanisms of ego defence are carried to extremes that they constitute abnormal behaviour.

A common defence and an obvious tactic against situations which provoke high anxiety is withdrawal. Withdrawal can take various forms; individuals may withdraw by physically absenting themselves or by having little verbal or non-verbal contact with other people. Daydreaming is, of course, a common form of escape. Withdrawal can also take the form of lack of commitment or of apparent unconcern towards a particular activity. Much withdrawal is perfectly normal and this is particularly the case when adults demand too much of a child and he feels overwhelmed. In this case withdrawal is healthy self-protection.

Another frequently used defence is projection. This is the

tendency for an individual to avoid personal blame for his difficulties and to put the blame elsewhere. Avoidance of personal blame is, in effect, an assertion that blame must be placed on someone or something else. Thus, in this sense, the individual projects his own responsibility or guilt on to other people or other factors. With a child or student failing in school, for example, there is sometimes the tendency to criticize the teachers, the subject matter, the buildings, etc. The author has witnessed countless instances of projection behaviour among aspiring junior lawn tennis champions who are often under immense pressure from parents and coaches to succeed. The court surface is blamed, the wind, the racquets, the balls, the spectators, the linesmen and the umpire. Most people use projection to some degree at some time and, as with other mechanisms of ego defence, the practice only becomes of serious concern when carried to an extreme when people may have delusions of persecution or of paranoia. However, even the use of projection to a mild degree tends to lower concentration for a particular event and accordingly has an adverse effect on performance. This point is discussed more fully in the section in Chapter 4 which discusses the problem of concentration.

A further widely used mechanism of ego defence is that of regression. Regressing to a more primitive mode of response or of behaviour occurs when an individual is confronted by difficulties and frustrations to the extent that he simply 'gives up' and may actually say so out loud. The reactions may take the form of weeping, kicking or throwing objects, stamping the feet and various other indications of frustration, fear and anger. Thus, in the examination room a candidate may simply do nothing positive about answering the questions and may just casually flick through the papers. Regressive behaviour may perhaps release physical tension and help us 'to get things out of our system' but it seldom solves any problems.

Rationalization is a common form of defence and it is used mainly to try to explain away failures. It is a device which we use not only to convince other people but also ourselves. People may put forward reasons or, more accurately, excuses for their failure. Sportsmen may say that they were not really bothered or interested to account for their defeat; students who do badly in a particular subject in an examination may say that they were concentrating their efforts on other subjects which had greater appeal and provided better opportunities vocationally. This preserves self-esteem, the implication being that if the student did try, if he were interested, the result would have been different. In tennis tournaments, for example, it is quite common at present for defeated players to announce that 'it was difficult to get interested'. Rationalization may take the form of placing blame. Thus, in tennis, players frequently blame the racquet, the court, the wind or the noise. Examinations provide many examples of this form of rationalization. We hear that the questions were not fair, that there was too much noise or, in examinations involving a public performance, that the judges were biased.

Mechanisms of ego defence operate, therefore, when people become frustrated and overanxious. Defences tend to be widely used when individuals are under prolonged and considerable stress. With respect to examinations, defence mechanisms often indicate a negative approach and can seriously disrupt concentration since attention is often directed away from the task in hand.

The relationship between anxiety and performance

The relationship between anxiety and performance has been investigated extensively by psychologists for many years. Studies were carried out by the Americans Yerkes and Dodson in 1908 and their findings were verified by numerous subsequent studies. These show that there is an optimum level of anxiety for maximum performance with both low and high levels of anxiety being associated with relatively poor standards of performance. Performance improves up to an optimum beyond which there is a decline. This law, therefore, considers that the relationship between anxiety and performance can be depicted as an inverted U-shaped curve with both high and low levels associated with poor performance; however, the position is generally not so simple. While the relationship between anxiety and performance is usually curvilinear, the precise relationship in any specific situation is dependent upon a number of variables which can interact with one another. Such factors as ability, the need for achievement, the presence of an audience, past experiences of similar situations, the adequacy of preparation and even the time of day (Blake, 1967) are all factors which can influence the nature of the relationship between anxiety and performance.

It is possible to distinguish between the types of mistakes which occur at either extreme of the anxiety continuum. At low levels of anxiety errors are generally those of omission with signals being lost in the perceptual system. Performance is poor because the individual is not alert and is not attending sufficiently to the task in hand. At high levels of anxiety errors tend to be those of commission. Performance is disrupted and behaviour is disorganized because the system is overactive.

As described in Chapter 1, Welford (1968) has suggested that performance improves as the anxiety level increases because impulses from the brain render the cortex more sensitive and responsive. He considers that the decline of performance at very high levels of anxiety is due to an intense stream of impulses from the brain stem causing the cells in the cortex to fire which results in the signals becoming blurred, cells normally used for carrying messages becoming refractory and the capacity of the brain being accordingly lowered. Hence, high levels of anxiety could inhibit performance on more difficult and complex tasks, though performance of relatively simple tasks is unaffected and can indeed be facilitated by high activation. Therefore, a high level of anxiety impairs the intense concentration which is needed for doing well in tests and examinations.

Research by Weiner et al. (1972) indicates the differential effects of past experience upon performance. Weiner's findings indicated that highly anxious individuals improved following initial success. If, however, they did poorly at first, subsequent performances declined. However, low-anxious people improved following initial failure but declined following initial success. These findings underline the need for assessing anxiety in some way for careful monitoring of progress and to assist the teacher in motivating students on a differential basis. The research indicates the motivational consequences of perceived task success or failure.

It is not uncommon for even experienced sportsmen to feel nervous before an important event. The famous English footballer Sir Stanley Matthews, is reported as saying that he still felt nervous before a big match even after some 25 years of First Division football. Most people, however, report that they feel far less nervous once the game gets under way and 'nerves' gradually cease to become much of a hindrance. People tend to become less nervous once the game begins partly because of the physical energy being expended which serves to reduce nervous tension and partly because they are now involved and concentrating on the game and the 'waiting is over'.

The evidence from research is that anxiety levels vary prior to, during and after competition. It is generally found, for example, that anxiety is relatively high before competition, as is shown in Figure 2. This situation seems to arise because people worry about how they will perform and the possibility of defeat or failure. Research findings (Hanin, 1978) support the view that once the competition begins anxiety levels for the majority of people begin to fall. It is also the case that the more physically demanding the event the more quickly do

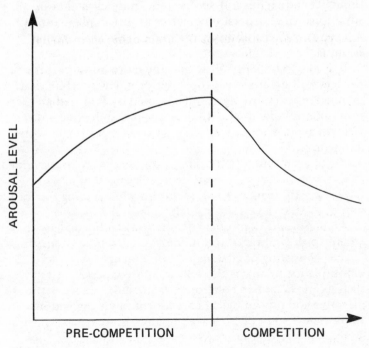

Figure 2 *Anxiety arousal levels prior to and during competition*

anxiety levels fall. This knowledge may not be of much comfort for the examination candidate who is 'tied' to his seat but the reference is made for its implications regarding the stress reduction techniques which are available for the overanxious candidate. To be exact, one way of lowering anxiety levels is to engage in some fairly vigorous physical activity in order to induce mild fatigue.

Wine (1971) considered that the low-anxious person attends mainly to the task and to a lesser extent to task-irrelevant variables. The high-anxious person, on the other hand, although attending to the task, is considerably distracted by task-irrelevant stimuli. Wine also showed that high-anxious people tended to be self-critical, self-preoccupied and self-dissatisfied. Test situations evoke negative, self-orientated responses which interfere with task concentration. In other words, the high test-anxious person is reacting to his thoughts and emotions rather than to the demands of the examination situation itself. His attention tends to become more and more focused on his own internal thoughts and feelings. It seems to be quite clear that in situations which a person perceives as threatening, anxiety interferes with the ability to attend to relevant external stimuli.

It seems to be fairly clear that the more important the test the less well do anxious people perform. High test-anxious people are also more adversely affected by failure than are low-anxious individuals. Anxious people, following a reverse, tend on average to do badly and in some cases to get worse and worse.

It has been found that failure experiences are best avoided in the case of the anxious student. It seems that anxiety levels rise still higher in failure groups while among successful groups anxiety levels show a fall.

An important theoretical distinction can be made with regard to the nature of test anxiety. This can be conceptualized as consisting of two major components: worry and emotionality. Worry is the self-orientated, pessimistic, distracting, cognitive component and emotionality is the affective and physiological component involving various unpleasant feelings which accompany a state of nervousness. In numerous studies the worry component has been shown to depress performance. Emotionality, on the other hand, does not seem to be directly related to performance decrement. Debilitating anxiety affects the student months — perhaps years — before the examination.

Sarason in a series of studies (1960, 1961) showed that the performance of low-anxious and high-anxious people was influenced by certain 'situational factors'. For instance, high-anxious people do worse than low-anxious people when the importance of doing well in an examination is emphasized. Sarason also found that the academic perform- ance of high-anxious people is enhanced when they are given instructions designed to reduce anxiety. However, the effect of such advice on low-anxious subjects is a lowering of performance levels. On the basis of his research Sarason considers that test-anxious people are more 'self-critical and more self-centred' than people who are low on test anxiety. As a result of their attitudes towards examinations, Sarason found that test-anxious people tend in the actual examination to be involved in a lot of negative self-talk which interferes considerably with attention and concentration. Examples of such negative self-talk or statements which have come to the attention of the author are:

— 'I just never have any luck with the questions'
— 'All this work for nothing'
— 'What on earth will people say?'
— 'This is the very last examination I take'
— 'I just give up'
— 'This is absolutely hopeless'.

High-anxious people do badly in tests for which it is diffi- cult to prepare, such as aptitude tests. Some examinations for the Civil Service, for example, include papers containing items or questions that are quite novel and for which it is virtually impossible to make any kind of preparation. In such situations high-anxious people are generally likely to fare badly. For these students novelty becomes equated with difficulty. The problem for the highly anxious person is that he habituates more slowly to stimuli. He takes longer to adjust, to become orientated, to situations. In new situations it is the uncertainty which causes the difficulty. This arises because in a new situation there can be some doubt about knowing what to do, what is expected and what is the correct or best course of action to take. In novel situations, for example, such as at a gathering for a course or meeting, people will start looking around to see how others are responding. Indeed, in order to allay anxiety and make people feel comfortable, there is often an invitation to sherry at the commencement of many meetings and courses. In the examination situation, however, such social pleasantries are not possible and people often feel very much on their own and are left to their own devices. It is a case of 'every man for himself'.

Highly anxious people also tend to do relatively poorly in the important examinations such as 'finals'. In the intermediate and less important examinations they tend to do better. In the mock examinations which 'don't count' they may even do quite well. But in highly stressful competitive situations they generally fare badly. Test situations which involve 'working against the clock' are difficult for the anxious student who may lose control of the situation and may experience feelings of 'being rushed'. Examinations which call for a public performance of some kind are difficult for the anxious student who is vulnerable to 'stage fright', for example. High-anxious people, in fact, tend to do particularly badly when being watched.

The 'climate' of the examination situation can also exert its influence on performance and serve further to discriminate between the performance of low- and high-anxious students. The greater the 'test-like' characteristics of the situation the worse high-anxious people will perform. In less test-like situations high-anxious people will tend to do better; they also do better in situations which provide cues to correct answers. The attitude and conduct of the invigilator are further factors. Thus instructions to the effect 'you will not be allowed to ask any questions', tend to increase the tenseness of the situation.

Test anxiety

Introduction

Test anxiety is a major problem for large numbers of students. Examinations discriminate unfairly against the anxious person. Unfortunately for the test-anxious person the prevailing view in education is that examination stress is something which is almost inevitable. Examinations are generally seen as being just part of school and college life and students are expected to be able to cope with examination pressures. Of particular concern to the parents and teachers is the problem of the reasonably able and committed student who does well in his course work throughout the year but invariably 'falls down' when it comes to the examinations. The position for many families as the 'examination season' approaches each year can become rather desperate.

The concepts of anxiety viewed as a trait (A-trait) and anxiety viewed as a state (A-state) have considerable significance for academic performance. As we have seen, trait anxiety is the stable, enduring aspect of personality. It is the predisposition of individuals to behave in a more or less anxious way over a wide range of situations. Generally speaking, people with high levels of trait anxiety are more likely to exhibit high state anxiety in more situations than people with low trait anxiety. High trait-anxious individuals perceive more situations as threatening to their self-esteem. Thus trait anxiety is a latent disposition to behave in a more or less anxious way in stressful situations. With respect to examinations it is likely that some students will be generally anxious in many situations and others will be generally less anxious. However, it is also the case that some students with high trait anxiety may show high levels of anxiety in some subjects but not in others as a result of their ability and previous successful experiences. On the other hand, students with low trait anxiety could be at ease with most subjects but could feel intense anxiety when faced with an examination in a subject for which they had a poor record. It might also be the case that a previous examination had involved a public performance of some kind which had been an embarrassing failure. Thus, in this case a student may become 'conditioned' to experience feelings of anxiety in subsequent examinations of a similar kind.

Test anxiety and performance

The early research in the 1950s by Mandler and Sarason (1952, 1953) demonstrated that test anxiety invariably resulted in a deterioration in performance in test-evaluative

51

situations. However, test anxiety does not affect all students equally. Students of very high ability are generally not affected, nor are students at the opposite extreme of the ability range. It is the vast majority of students in the middle range of ability whose performance is likely to be depressed. For students of high ability, examinations clearly create less arousal because they are perceived as being less difficult than is the case for students of only average ability. Sarason and Mandler consider that the test evaluative situation elicits drives which are task relevant and also anxiety drives — some of which are task relevant and some irrelevant. Both drives are *learned*. Task-relevant and anxiety-relevant drives facilitate performance. On the other hand, anxiety drives which are irrelevant impair performance. Anxiety is debilitating and the performance of the highly anxious person is lowered in the examination situation. These researchers argue that the highly anxious individual worries during examinations, and may even engage in day-dreaming to some extent. As a result concentration can be seriously affected.

Test anxiety: assessment

A number of self-report tests have been developed to assess test anxiety. The first test to be published was the Test Anxiety Questionnaire (TAQ) by Mandler and Sarason in 1952. The test was designed to assess the anxiety feelings of adults engaged in examinations. A test for high school children, the Test Anxiety Scale (TAS) was later developed from the TAQ. Both tests are concerned with a person's reported feelings and stress reactions in the testing situation. The items, for example, are concerned with emotional feelings of uneasiness, worry cognitions and physiological indices of arousal such as heartbeat and perspiration. Another self-report measure is the Test Anxiety Behaviour Scale (TABS) developed by Suin in 1969. Liebert and Morris produced the Worry-Emotionality Questionnaire in 1967; this test is concerned with assessing a student's immediate feelings. The Test Anxiety Inventory (TAI) developed by Spielberger et al. (1978) is based on the theory that test anxiety is essentially a situation-specific form of trait anxiety. The test is short, having only 20 items, but high correlations are reported with the well-established tests in this area. The TAI uses a four-point scale and separate scores can be obtained

References

Blake, M. J. F. (1967). Relationship between circadian rhythm of body temperature and introversion — extroversion. *Nature*. 215, 896-7.

Fenz, W. D. and Epstein, S. (1969) Stress in the air. *Psychology Today*. 27-8 and 58-9.

Freud, S. (1962) *The Complete Works of Sigmund Freud*. Hogarth, London.

Hanin, Y. L. (1978) A study of anxiety in sports. In Straub, W. F. (ed.) *Sport Psychology*. Mouvement Publications, New York.

Liebert, R. M. and Morris, L. W. (1967) Cognitive and emotional components of test anxiety. A distinction and some initial data. *Psychological Reports 1967*. 20, 975-8.

Main, A. (1980) *Encouraging Effective Learning*. Scottish Academic Press, Edinburgh.

Mandler, G. and Sarason, S. B. (1952) A study of anxiety and learning. *Journal of Abnormal and Social Psychology*. 47, 166-173.

Mandler, G. and Sarason, S. B. (1953) The effect of prior experience and subjective failure on the evocation of test anxiety. *Journal of Personality*. 21, 336-41.

Meichenbaum, D. H. (1972) Cognitive modification of test anxious college students. *Journal of Consulting & Clinical Psychology*. 39, 370-80.

Sarason, I. G. (1960) Empirical findings and theoretical problems in the use of anxiety scales. *Psychological Bulletin*. 57, 403-15.

Sarason, I. G. (1961) Test anxiety and intellectual performance. *Journal of Educational Psychology*. 52, 201-6.

Sarason, I. G. (1978) The Test Anxiety Scale. In C. D. Spielberger and I. G. Sarason (eds) *Stress and Anxiety*. 5. Hemisphere, Washington.

Spielberger, C. D. (1978) *The Test Anxiety Inventory*.

Spielberger, C. D., Gorsuch, R. L. and Lushane, R. E. (1970) *Manual for the State-Trait Anxiety Inventory*. Consulting Psychologist Press, Palo Alto, California.

Suin, R. M. (1969) Test Anxiety Behaviour Scale. *Behaviour Research and Therapy*. 7, 335-9.

Tryon, G. S. (1980) The Measurement and Treatment of Test Anxiety. *Review of Educational Research*. 50 (2), 343-72.

Weiner, B. et al. (1972) Perceiving the causes of success and failure. In E. E. Jones et al. (eds) *Attribution: Perceiving the causes of behaviour.* General Learning Press, Morristown.

Welford, A. T. (1968) *Fundamentals of skill*. Methuen, London.

Wine, J. (1971) Test anxiety and direction of attention. *Psychological Bulletin.* 76, 92-104.

Yerkes, R. and Dodson, J. (1908) The relation of strength of stimulus to rapidity of habit formation. *Journal of Comparative Neurology and Psychology.* 18, 459-82.

Chapter 3

Stress

Stress is a state that disrupts the homeostasis or internal
equilibrium of the body. It can be defined as the demands
the environment places on an individual and can be viewed
from the standpoint of testing man in much the same way as
testing machines. Prior to the Second World War, stress was
essentially an engineering term but later it increasingly came
to be used to refer to the psychological and physical demands
which are made on people. Stress is difficult to define
because individuals differ remarkably in their reactions to
particular situations. It is, therefore, more helpful to talk of
perceived stress. The term perceived stress is used because
people vary in the extent to which they see a particular event
as being stressful. The degree of perceived stress is an important factor to consider. The term perceived stress is employed
because the degree of stress attached to a specific situation
is dependent, to a considerable extent, on the perceptions
of the individual which are the product of his emotional
disposition, his previous experiences of similar situations,
his abilities, the importance of the event and the need to
achieve. It is the individual's interpretation of the situation
and his own feelings which determine the degree of stress.
Thus situations which are seen as threatening to a person's
self-esteem and prestige can give rise to greater feelings of
anxiety than situations which might involve actual physical
harm. This serves to underline the point that it is not just
the objective situation which causes anxiety but the individual's subjective assessment of the situation. The position
is further complicated by the fact that the perception
of stress, even for the same person, can vary from one
competitive event to another and even, over time, for one
and the same event. Stress is generally considered from two

standpoints. It is viewed with respect to situations or conditions which are sources of stress or it is viewed with respect to the individual's responses or reactions to stress. When the situation or condition is referred to, the terms stressor or agent are generally used.

Stressors, or agents which induce stress, generally come in the form of incentives, and increasing the incentive, increasing the importance of the event for the individual, increases the stress. Rewards and punishments are stressful agents as is the presence of spectators or an audience. Competitive situations such as interviews, speaking at debates, sitting examinations, meeting new people and starting a new job, are all stressful when a person perceives them as threatening, (threatening, that is, to his prestige, self-esteem or physical welfare). The stimuli which cause the most stress are those which are novel, very intense or signals of danger, because it is to these that habituation least easily occurs. More generally, arousal level is raised by any task which is in some way challenging, which demands an effort, and by anything which acts as an incentive. With respect to tests of performance, such as examinations, stress reactions will be closely related to the extent of any difference which may exist between the perceived demands of the test and an individuals's perception of his own capabilities. For motivated students the greater the gap the greater will be the pressure and worry for the person. Further, stress reactions are very likely to be experienced by the inadequate performer both during the test and afterwards.

Reactions to stress are highly individualistic and are dependent on a large number of factors. Much depends on an individual's predisposition to react to stressful stimuli by reason of his personality. Research has concentrated on two broad variations. These are the habitual, normal or chronic level of arousal on the one hand, and the speed and extent to which arousal levels rise with the introduction of stress on the other. Thus introverted people, who are generally more highly activated than extroverted people, and neurotic individuals who are relatively easily aroused, are vulnerable to stressful conditions. It is indeed the case that nervous tense individuals have a low tolerance for stress both physically and psychologically. Stable, calm, temperamentally robust individuals, on the other hand, can withstand greater degrees of stress and tend to perform better under stressful conditions than under normal circumstances.

In addition to personality predispositions an individual's response to stress will be influenced by his past experiences and, in particular, his past experiences of similar situations. Stress reactions can be influenced by a series of unpleasant, discomforting experiences and also by a single traumatic experience. However, repeated exposure to a stressful situation may enable a person to habituate to that stress and to learn to cope with it more effectively. This can be the case provided that the stress tolerance level is not greatly exceeded. However, it is not always so. Research by Eysenck and Rachman (1965) indicates that emotional problems can arise as a result of a series of stressful experiences rather than one traumatic event. The situation is complex and, as has already been indicated, is influenced not only by situational factors but by factors within the individual, such as his personality and past experiences of similar situations.

Stress is now regarded by many as being an event that requires some adjustment and accommodation on the part of the individual. Examinations are stressful because they frequently exert pressures on people which call for more than ordinary effort. Pressures can be particularly great, for example, during an examination that involves some kind of public performance. From the student's viewpoint a major source of stress is the threat to self-esteem and the loss of status and prestige which would follow a poor examination result. A decrease in self-esteem leads to feelings and sensations of unhappiness, disorganization and anxiety. Increases in self-esteem, on the other hand, are frequently accompanied by feelings of happiness, enthusiasm and freedom. An individual's perception of a stressful or threatening situation usually results in increased anxiety accompanied by an elevation of physiological measures of arousal, such as an increase in heart rate and sweating. Behavioural indications might include restlessness and a general tenseness of posture.

For teachers, counsellors, therapists and students who are interested in stress management strategies and techniques, it might be helpful at this point to make a brief survey of the nature of stress and stress responses.

Reactions to stress

The main physiological, behavioural and cognitive reactions to stress are discussed below. It will be noted that anxiety almost invariably underlies an individual's reactions to stress. Frequently, for most people, there is also an increase in muscular tension. Marked variations occur in individual reactions to stress; for example, although there is an increase in muscular tension for most people, some become tense in most muscle groups while others become tense only in some. Again, heart rate rises sharply in the case of some individuals while in others there is hardly any change. Breathing generally tends to become more rapid and shallow though even this response is not universal. Although marked differences exist between individuals in their reactions to stress, the stress reactions for one and the same person are remarkably consistent over a wide range of situations to the extent that close relatives, friends, teachers and coaches will often recognize the symptoms of stress and realize that the person is under pressure of some kind. Inwardly, for example, a person might always experience a sinking feeling or have cold hands when facing an intimidating situation.

Bodily responses

Bodily reactions to stress can include an increase in heart rate, shortness of breath, trembling hands, shaking legs, palpitations, nausea, sweating, pallor and actual fainting in some cases. These reactions are an indication that the body is preparing itself for action and patterns of reactions which occur among people under threat are sometimes referred to as indicative of the Fight or Flight Syndrome.

A number of bodily reactions to stress can be measured, such as heart rate, blood pressure and sweating, and can provide important information concerning a person's vulnerability and reaction to stressors. For example, many people under stress begin to sweat and indices commonly used to measure levels of arousal are skin conductance and the galvanic skin response. It is the galvanic skin response which is used to indicate a person's temporary state of activation or tension as a stress response. Bodily reactions are related to emotional states and bodily reactions to stress can influence emotional reactions and vice versa.

Emotional and behavioural responses

The emotional reactions to stress or to threatening situations can be decidedly unpleasant. These may be feelings of apprehension, dread, uncertainty, self-doubt, blame and worries about inadequacies and shortcomings. Occasionally there can be an alarming feeling of losing control and, in the extreme, feelings of terror and panic. Behavioural reactions might include restlessness and fidgeting, with a tendency to become generally tense and jumpy. The behaviour of a person who is under stress tends to become rigid, inflexible and stereotyped with a failure to adapt to, or even to perceive, changing conditions in situations.

Performance responses

Severe stress invariably results in a deterioration in the performance of complex, difficult tasks whether these be verbal, non-verbal or motor. There is a lowering of attention and concentration with people sometimes becoming confused and disorganized. At heightened levels of anxiety and stress, attention becomes increasingly internally focused rather task-orientated; for example, people may start to worry about failing. Self-centred, interfering thoughts distract attention from the task and result in a deterioration of performance. As with behaviour, cognitive functioning generally tends to be rigid, with a failure to perceive and respond to subtle changes in the demands of examination questions for example. Cognitive functioning can become inhibited by negative self-talk when people are working under extreme pressure. Such statements as 'Oh, this is too difficult for me', 'I can't remember', 'I can't think', 'I don't know which one to do', 'I won't bother again', 'I never was any good at examinations', etc, are indicative of the pressure a person is working under. He therefore becomes confused concerning the appropriate action to take.

Stress and performance

People generally perform best under intermediate conditions of stress. It is at the two extremes of high and low levels of stress that individuals do least well. This is because the introduction of stress to a learning situation, in the form of competition or of various incentives, involves action of the autonomic nervous system with an increase in the level of arousal. As with anxiety, performance improves as the arousal level increases to an optimum, following which it begins to decline. Performance improves as the arousal level increases because the individual becomes more alert and can respond to events more quickly and accurately. Thus mild stress is generally associated with an improvement in performance and severe stress with a fall in performance due to individuals becoming over-aroused. Occasionally, under very severe stress, individuals panic and there is a breakdown in learning and a regression to a more primitive or earlier form of response or lower level of skill.

Experience and performance

We have already referred to the fact that experience is a predisposing factor in an individual's reactions to stress. The following section is concerned with an individual's past experience of stressful situations or activities and how these relate to current performance.

Stress and examination performance

Examinations represent a measure of performance under stress. Public examinations commonly constitute one of the most extreme forms of competition in contemporary society. The psychological pressures can be immense. It is evident that the greater the stress, the greater the need to succeed, the more important do emotional factors become in determining examination performance. Severe stress affects overanxious people in different ways. As has already been discussed, some become tense and rigid, others become very active but in an ineffective way. Attention becomes increasingly internally focused when it should be exclusively externally focused, that is on the set questions and how they should be answered. The candidate is often hesitant, indecisive and becomes trapped in his own negative internally-focused thoughts concerning the social consequences of failure. The effects, therefore, of highly stressful conditions on the performance of the overanxious, over-activated candidate can be devastating. In both states there is a deterioration in functioning intelligence. Some people 'freeze' and write very little indeed while others panic and respond with an 'everything except the kitchen sink' approach and fail to respond specifically to the question; still others avoid the examination altogether.

Experience of stress

The popular notion concerning the experience of stressful situations is that people must derive some psychological benefit and as a result become 'tougher' in a temperamental sense and be able to perform better in competitive situations. Thus we read of hardened, 'battle-seasoned' troops in war and of professional sportsmen who have undergone the rigours of demanding world tours and are considered to have been 'toughened up' by the experience. However, exposing people to stressful experiences does not always have the desired, anticipated training effect. Research by Eysenck and Rachman (1965), for example, indicates that far from 'toughening' people a series of noxious or stressful experiences can lead to emotional problems and even to neurotic breakdown in some soldiers during warfare. Again, Welford (1967) refers to the effects of prolonged exposure to stress in airline pilots and why it is that as a result of this experience they may become less efficient and more accident prone.

With respect to the relationship between the experience of an activity and the resulting stress reactions, some interesting work has been carried out by Walter Fenz of the University of Waterloo in Canada. Fenz worked with parachute jumpers and studied stress reactions in relation to experience and ability. In this particular activity the stress of the situation is extreme since life itself is at risk.

This research shows that not only were there differences in the stress responses of experienced and novice jumpers as indicated by physiological measures of arousal, but marked differences also existed between experienced parachuters of high ability and those of low ability. Successful, experienced jumpers, although having elevated levels of arousal on the morning of the event, were able to reduce this level to just above the normal resting state immediately prior to the jump. In some way they had been able to develop coping strategies to offset the stress of the situation. On the other hand, in the case of both the unsuccessful, experienced jumper and the novice, arousal levels continued to remain high right up to the moment of the jump. This research underlines the point that experience of a situation may either be beneficial or detrimental to future performance. Successive experiences of parachute jumping do not necessarily serve to reduce arousal levels to an optimum level for successful performance.

The position is further complicated by evidence that poor test performance leads to rather higher levels of performance in subsequent tests by low-anxious subjects, but that the reverse is true for high-anxious students whose performances become worse and worse following initial failure (Mandler and Sarason, 1952). Mandler and Sarason argue that high levels of anxiety evoke responses which are incompatible with successful performance such as feelings of inadequacy and helplessness, and worry about public censure.

However, although most people are often very well prepared intellectually and academically for examinations, and physically for sporting qualifications, systematic psychological preparation in the affective domain remains virtually non-existent. The traditional view is that emotional adjustment is something which will come with experience or you simply 'don't have what it takes' and there is nothing much which can be done about it. This 'survival of the fittest' approach pervades the professional scene in a number of sports. Such slogans as 'When the going gets tough, the tough get going' and 'Defeat is worse than death. You have to live with defeat', which appear on the walls of some changing rooms in the USA typify this approach. Again, to take another example from sport, in tennis there is the belief that continual competitive play guarantees effective performance and progress. The reverse often happens and what in fact is generated is a very high level of unnecessary stress which serves in the end to undermine even the performance of the temperamentally robust. Not surprisingly many promising young players at the age of around 16 years old abandon the game altogether for less harrowing pursuits.

In the academic field the practice in many schools is to give young people as much experience of examinations as is possible in the belief that they will gain from such experience. The gains to be had are discussed at length in Chapter 5 in the section which deals with the function of practice tests.

The presence of an audience

Some tests and examinations involve a performance which is assessed by a panel of judges or interviewers. The effects on performance of the presence of spectators and critics have received extensive investigation.

The audience effect

Social facilitation, or the study of the audience effect on learning and performance, shows that even the mere presence of people will elicit a dominant response. The findings show that many factors can be involved and that an audience can have quite a dramatic effect upon standards. Sometimes performance is enhanced, sometimes it deteriorates and sometimes there is little discernible difference. The general effect of the audience is to raise arousal levels. This facilitates performance of simple and well-learned tasks but tends to disrupt performance of difficult or slightly learned tasks; this is particularly so in the case of anxious individuals. Zajoric (1965) argues that an important distinction can be made between performance and learning. He considers that with an audience present the dominant response is facilitated. Thus the presence of an audience will tend to inhibit learning because the person has not learned a single, correct response but has a wide range of incorrect responses that are dominant and these are facilitated. After the learner has acquired the skill correctly the presence of an audience should enhance performance by facilitating the emission of this learned dominant response. Thus according to Zajoric the presence of an audience generally tends to inhibit learning but to enhance performance. It is considered that it is probably advisable to follow Zajoric's thinking and that the best skill-learning environment does not contain an audience. The nature of the relationship between spectators and a person's performance is a complex one and is determined by the particular factors involved in any one specific situation and the several ways in which they may combine and interact with one another. Two broad groups of factors are readily identified: those which relate to the individual in terms of his experience, ability, motivation and personality, and those which relate to the actual composition of the audience in terms of status, knowledge, size and sex.

Generally speaking, the performance of stable and extroverted people tends to improve before an audience and that of anxious and introverted people to decline. It is, in fact, perfectly possible for anxious people to be doing better on average than stable people when they are not being watched, but for the position to be completely reversed when an audience is introduced, with stable people now doing that much better and anxious people that much worse (Figure 3).

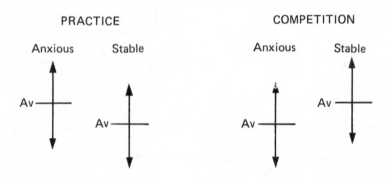

Figure 3 *Performance of anxious and stable subjects during practice and during competition*

The effects of an audience on performance are also related to ability, with superior individuals doing better when watched and mediocre or moderate individuals tending to do worse than when they are unobserved. Indeed, superior games players at international level are frequently inspired to do better in front of a large crowd and actually to revel in the atmosphere. It is as though they really need the excitement generated by an enthusiastic crowd to reach the supreme heights of play of which they are capable. Denis Compton, for example, the great England Test cricketer of the immediate post-war era is reported as saying that he was not interested in playing if he was only going to be watched by 'two men and a dog'. In tennis there are clearly a number of players who manifestly enjoy the experience of playing before a capacity crowd on the centre court at Wimbledon and greatly prefer this to the relative quiet of the outside courts.

For the highly motivated person the composition of the audience in terms of its perceived status can be a highly stressful factor. Thus the presence of selectors and judges or examiners is likely to be a stressful experience for most young people. The author had firsthand experience of this situation when conducting motor skill tests in schools. Upon the appearance of the headmaster, sometimes accompanied by a visting Inspector of Schools, there would be quite sharp changes in perfoŗmance with some boys performing far better and others far worse. It seems likely, therefore, that the more acute the stress, the more dramatic is the change in performance.

For the majority of people engaged in examinations there will always be an audience regardless of whether there are people actually physically present or not. This 'hidden' audience will be the people who will be studying the results in the newspapers, namely relatives, teachers and various other social acquaintances. The 'hidden' audience is a stressor and can serve to distract attention from the task in hand.

Coaction

An audience might also be considered in terms of coaction. Coaction is when a number of people are engaged in the same activity at the same time. Here, in general, the effects of coaction are similar to those of a passive audience in that learning is impaired and performance enhanced. As with social facilitation, coaction is a complex process often involving a number of variables. With respect to problem solving, however, and tasks involving judgement, coaction tends to impair performance. The stress arising from coaction is influenced by both the proximity and the number of people engaged in the same activity. As might be expected, the closer the people and the larger the number, the greater are the coaction effects, producing generally higher levels of arousal. Thus people who are already optimally aroused for activity when performing a task are likely to become over-aroused to the detriment of performance when joined by others.

Coaction has been referred to because there are some students who find large examination halls and the presence of hundreds of other people to be a disturbing and unsettling experience. In the author's survey, for example, 3.5 per cent of students attributed their relatively poor performance to the 'presence of other people', and 34.5 per cent considered that they would have done better if they could have worked in private.

The management of stress

Introduction

The strategies and techniques which are reviewed in this section are also discussed in later chapters of the book. Although a highly individualized approach is frequently required in stress management, certain basic strategies and techniques can be identified which are generally employed to varying degrees. It is, of course, preferable in most situations to avoid exceeding a person's stress tolerance level. This is not easy although much stress is avoidable, and indeed is often unnecessary, in the everyday work of both schools and colleges. Prevention, of course, is better than cure. The problem is that people become conditioned to experiencing stress reactions whether or not they are warranted by the current situation. Furthermore, in many instances, people are convinced that this will always be the case. Verbal advice and suggestions used in isolation are often found to be a complete waste of time. Indeed, words of encouragement do nothing for the overanxious examinee in the same way as they do nothing for someone with a fear of flying.

It is important that people should learn to recognize the difference between a state of tension and a state of relaxation. It is important also to be able to recognize symptoms which predict the onset of tension and result in stress reactions. Recognition makes a person able to initiate prompt counter-alleviating measures. International athletes, for example, sometimes engage in relaxation exercises to reduce tension in the sports arena prior to the race. The problem is that preliminary emotional reactions to stress 'trigger off' bodily feelings and sensations which adversely affect concentration and these bodily reactions serve further to heighten feelings of anxiety. Thus a person can sometimes be caught in a 'downward spiral' with the reactions to stress becoming self-perpetuating; as is sometimes said, anxiety 'feeds on itself'.

Experience of stress and performance

Examination stress can be managed. Stress management programmes can be developed to meet the needs of individual students with test anxiety problems. The first stage of a stress management programme would be for students to learn something about the nature of stress, to be appraised of the common sources of stress and of the phsyiological, emotional, behavioural and cognitive reactions to stress. This educative phase would serve to give students greater self-awareness and also insight into, and an appreciation of, the purpose and functions of the strategies they would need to follow and the techniques they would need to practise in the management of stress. The ability to be physically relaxed yet mentally alert, and to work efficiently under pressure is a skill which can be acquired following a period of relevant, sustained, systematic practice. The section which follows outlines a number of strategies and techniques which can be effectively employed in the management of stress. They have all been employed in major research investigations concerned with the facilitation of learning and the enhancement of performance in test-evaluative situations.

1. Providing information

Uncertainty, as will generally be well appreciated from experience, is a potent source of stress. Doubts about the departure times of aeroplanes or trains, for example, soon lead to agitation and alarm among prospective travellers. Thus any programme concerned with the control of examination stress should aim to keep uncertainties concerning the event to a minimum.

There is some basic information which all students need to know, such as the date, time and duration of the examination, and the location of the centre where it is to take place. If the student does not know the centre it might be a good idea to make a visit and to become familiar with the place if this is possible. Details of the number of questions and the degree of choice available also need to be known.

Prospective candidates need to be given some idea of the criteria which are traditionally followed by the examiners in the assessment of scripts. The student needs to know what is important in the syllabus and what really needs to be studied; he needs to know what is expected of him in order to achieve a high grade. In this respect, it is important for a candidate to have information about his own current performance and how this specifically relates to the performance which is generally required to be successful. Any deficiency in performance needs to be pointed out and diagnosed, and suggested guidelines for improvement need to be outlined. Advice should be given on how to tackle the paper as a whole and how to tackle individual questions. Additionally, some candidates may need advice on how to study and how to develop intellectual capacities.

Evaluations are very important and not just for the grades alone. If they are thoroughly given, they point out the strengths and weaknesses in a student's work and provide him with valuable information concerning the direction and emphasis of future study. An individual may also need assistance with motivational and emotional problems if he is likely to experience difficulty in coping adequately with the stress of the examination. Such problems might emerge during mock examinations if the conditions are made sufficiently realistic. Information concerning test anxiety or examination stress can be obtained in a variety of ways. These include self-report inventories, observation, use of check lists, interviews and counselling; these are discussed extensively elsewhere in this book.

2. Relaxation

For the highly anxious person a major consideration is that he must learn how to relax for, in general, a state of relaxation is incompatible with discomforting feelings of anxiety. Progressive relaxation is a technique which is widely used in the reduction of stress. Being relaxed also assists concentration since attention is not distracted by uncomfortable feelings arising from muscular tension. The aim of a relaxation programme is for the state of relaxation to become a well-learned response with a person sensing that he is becoming increasingly in control of his feelings. Twenty minutes' practice a day for around three months is sufficient for most people to acquire this relaxation technique.

Relaxation can be defined as being a lower state of arousal than the normal waking state. Relaxation differs from sleep because during sleep, as in the waking state, arousal levels fluctuate. Sleep is a psyche-physiological state. Arousal levels in sleep are lower than in the normal waking state but fluctuations occur and are probably related in some way to the emotional intensity of the dreams which an individual may experience. In sleep, arousal levels can fluctuate above and below the generally stable arousal level produced by systematic relaxation. A state of relaxation also differs from the state which is produced by tranquillizing drugs. Drugs depress the senses; relaxation, on the other hand, heightens the awareness of bodily sensations while at the same time relaxing the body and mind. There are two main forms of relaxation training: centralized and peripheral. Centralized or psychosomatic forms begin with the mind, and peripheral or somatopsychic begin with the body. Examples of psycho-somatic approaches to relaxation include meditation, hypnosis and imaging. Somatopsychic techniques include progressive relaxation, various forms of breath control and biofeedback training, among others.

Progressive relaxation
Progressive muscle relaxation is a technique which was developed by Edward Jacobson in the early 1930s. Jacobson (1938) argued that people were often unaware of the physical tension in themselves. He theorized that by inducing muscular tension people would learn to recognize it. He considered that people could achieve greater awareness of tension and start learning to relax by alternately tensing and relaxing various muscles. Jacobson's technique involves systematic tension followed by relaxation of all the major muscle groups in the body. It is the case that when a muscle is tensed and is then relaxed it returns to a more relaxed state than formerly. Tensing the muscle really hard will produce a high level of relaxation in the muscle when it is subsequently relaxed.

Jacobson claimed success for his technique in the treatment of a variety of stress-related problems. These included the successful treatment of patients suffering from hypertension, anxiety neuroses, asthma and insomnia, among other conditions. Although some doubt exists concerning the validity of the claims with respect to some conditions, relaxation is the most widely used psychological technique in the treatment of insomnia today. In the majority of cases it is an effective and efficient technique for people with a sleep problem.

Progressive relaxation is particularly helpful to those who experience levels of anxiety and tension which exert an adverse influence on performance in test-evaluative situations such as academic examinations. Progressive relaxation is also being used on a systematic basis with some international athletes in order to give them greater control over both emotional and cognitive factors. With respect to research conducted with students and athletes, progressive muscular relaxation is frequently considered to be basic in programmes for the treatment of anxiety.

In the world of competitive sport progressive relaxation is increasingly being recognized as an essential part of the

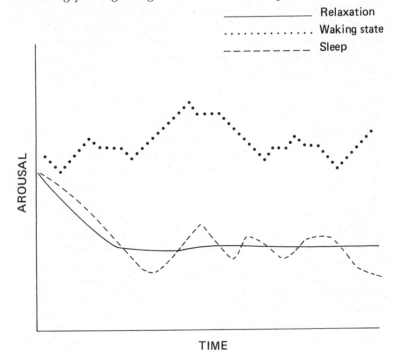

Figure 4 *Arousal patterns during waking states, sleep and systematic relaxation*

preparation programme of the athlete as he faces the rigours of competition at international level. Training in progressive relaxation is also beneficial in that it reduces the time which people expend worrying and ruminating about problems and shortcomings — eg in worrying about loss of sleep.

Learning to relax means that people are able to make more efficient use of the time they spend in study and practice. Progressive relaxation should be practised in conjunction with other stress-management techniques. The programme which is outlined later in this chapter is a modification of Jacobson's programme. Regular practice on a daily basis is important; the aim should be to practise progressive relaxation to the point where it becomes a well-learned response. For the test-anxious student the aim should be for relaxation to become the dominant response in stress situations such as examinations. The problem for the anxious student is that the test situation can elicit anxiety drives which can be either task relevant or task irrelevant. Task-irrelevant drives, such as worry, have debilitating effects and serve to lower performance. There is considerable evidence to the effect that relaxation training techniques are effective in reducing test anxiety and improving examination performance (Tryon, 1980). Relaxation improves concentration by reducing or eliminating worry cognitions. For the text-anxious student the importance of achieving the relaxation response cannot be overemphasized.

Relaxation programme

The overriding aim of the relaxation programme is for the state of relaxation to become a well-learned response so that the negative effects of anxiety are replaced by the positive benefits of relaxation, which come in the form of developing confidence and greater efficiency with the student's mind now working for him rather than against him. The programme is based upon Edmund Jacobson's progressive deep muscle relaxation procedure which he developed in 1938. A relaxation programme should be seen as a central feature of the total achievement strategy. For example, in tennis, if a player is to perform to the best of his ability in a match, he needs to be mentally alert yet at the same time physically loose and relaxed — 'as loose as ashes' as one American author once put it. When relaxed and comfortable, people tire less easily because less energy is dissipated than when in a tense and agitated state. Some players become so tense before and during a match that they suffer from headaches and stomach cramps arising from prolonged, excessive tension. Physical pain is likely to disrupt performance through a lowering of concentration and through fatigue. Indeed, some players are both mentally and physically tired before the match even starts.

Relaxation exercises can help a person entering a stressful situation to be in a calm physical condition. Completely relaxing muscles, particularly those of the forehead, eyes and face, induces sleep, improves digestion and reduces those bodily pains which have their origins in exposure to excessive degrees of stress. The programme is based upon the knowledge that body and mind states are interrelated and that uncomfortable anxiety sensations and feelings can be alleviated, and sometimes removed entirely, by reducing muscular tension. The following is a short programme of instructions designed to help bring about physical relaxation.

Make yourself comfortable in an easy chair. Close your eyes and go as limp as you can, let the weight in your body go completely, let your arms and legs feel heavy, like sandbags. Relax completely, start to breathe deeply and slowly, deeply and slowly, deeply and slowly. Become consciously aware of the rhythmic pattern of your breathing, thinking only of this as you breathe deeply and slowly, deeply and slowly. Continue for five minutes or so until you feel refreshed.

People are often unaware of the physical tension in themselves. You can achieve greater awareness of the tension in your body by alternately tensing and relaxing various muscles. Beginning with the right hand clench it very hard for a few seconds and then relax. Repeat again, clenching the hand, holding the tension and then relaxing. Now clench your right hand again but this time not so hard, feeling the difference in the lower tension level before relaxing again. Now, with the palm of your right hand facing downwards, stretch your fingers outwards and upwards. Feel the tension and then relax. Repeat the procedure again, stretching the fingers for a few moments before relaxing. Stretch your fingers outwards and upwards again, but this time not as far so that you feel that the tension is less. Now, perform these exercises with your left hand, clenching, stretching, holding for a few seconds and then relaxing. You should next proceed in turn to alternately tensing and relaxing the muscles in your forehead, neck and face, upper arms and shoulders, forearms, calves and thighs, and finally feet and toes. Try twisting your feet inwards and outwards. Next start to move your feet and toes upwards and back towards you, at the same time depressing your legs downwards. Finally turn to tensing the muscles in your stomach, chest and back.

You should now conclude your relaxation programme by spending a little time concentrating on tensing your whole body, holding the tension for a few seconds and then relaxing. Finally you can further deepen the level of relaxation by taking a deep breath on concluding the exercises. Doing these exercises will help you to recognize and sense the physical tension in various parts of your body and the extent to which you can become physically relaxed and more at ease mentally.

You will need to practice these exercises over and over again until you can relax at will and have control over the physical tension in your body. Some of the exercises can be done at odd times during the day, such as when waiting for a bus or train, or standing in a queue. Try, whenever possible, to use some of these exercises in situations which are stressful for you. You will need to persevere with them over a period of some weeks or maybe months, particularly if you are a rather anxious person, but they do work and are quite pleasant to perform. Practise the exercises every day and note the gradual improvement in your ability to reduce tension as you progress to the stage where you are a much more relaxed person generally. With extensive practice it becomes possible to relax within seconds.

Thus, relaxation is a skill which can be acquired through systematic practice over a period of several weeks. For people who are highly stressed the ability to achieve relaxation is important for test performance. Many people use self-induced relaxation (SIR) during actual performance.

3. Biofeedback training

Biofeedback training provides a person with important information concerning the physiology of the body. The use of biofeedback procedures can often speed up the process of learning to relax. One such procedure is to measure fingertip temperature before and after undertaking a programme of relaxation. In the more relaxed state, fingertip temperature will be raised because the flow of blood to the extremities of the body will be facilitated. The important point about a biofeedback procedure, such as the measurement of fingertip temperature, is that people do not have to rely on their own feelings or opinion as to their degree of relaxation. The reading on the thermometer gives people precise, objective and visual evidence of the progress they are making towards learning to relax; this means that they can relate what they do to what happens in terms of any change in fingertip temperature. Biofeedback training, therefore, provides people with information concerning how they have to practise and for how long, to get the best results. It is highly motivating because people are able to measure their progress and, therefore, they are frequently spurred on to improve both the depth of the relaxation response and the speed with which they are able to achieve it. An inexpensive hand thermometer is all that is needed although a digital thermometer, if available, will record even the slightest changes in fingertip temperature.

The importance of feedback for skill acquisition was emphasized in Chapter 1. People receiving feedback tend to pursue any task with greater application and diligence. Apart from its motivational value feedback does provide people with a yardstick by which to measure progress. Because of both its motivational and information value feedback is a crucial factor in both learning and performance. Biofeedback training provides a way of teaching people how to exert some degree of voluntary control over functions such as heart rate and blood pressure, which at one time were considered to be beyond voluntary control.

4. Accommodating to specific stress situations

Continued exposure to moderate or gradually increasing stress provides the opportunity for people to accommodate to stress and to learn how to handle it. It is important that individuals should gradually become acclimatized to the stressful situations which they will later encounter. The emotional demands of practice tests or examinations should be gradually built up so that the student learns to deal with increasing pressure. Emotional capacities can be developed by operating a system of handicaps, rewards or penalites which appropriately meet the needs of individual students. In the final stages of preparation practice sessions should duplicate the conditions which operate for the examination proper. Anxiety and arousal levels are at their highest before, and at the beginning of, an event. It is important to have a well-rehearsed routine concerning the procedure to be followed at the beginning of an examination. This serves to minimize uncertainty and to reduce indecision which is a common feature of the stress response.

5. Overlearning

A further step in the management of stress is to ensure that the subject matter or the skilled activity has been thoroughly learned — overlearned, in fact — which means learning far more than is necessary for one correct answer or performance. A good example to illustrate the term overlearning is to be found in learning to drive a car. People do not stop driving once they have passed the test but continue to drive on a regular daily basis; gradually the skill becomes overlearned to the extent that it is automatic and people forget what they actually do. This is evident when a person attempts to teach somebody how to change gear, for example — some thought is needed to discover what movements are actually made! A thorough knowledge of the subject or a complete mastery of the skilled activity also serves to reduce anxiety because the candidate now perceives the examination as being less difficult.

6. Intrinsic motivation

A further strategy which can be followed in the management of stress is to enhance intrinsic motivation. With intrinsically-motivated people the principal interest or concern is in the subject rather than in social considerations such as a higher salary or a better job which are seen as being of secondary importance. It can be argued that intrinsically-motivated people are in a better position emotionally to withstand frustrations and temporary set-backs. Following a reverse they become primarily concerned with analysing their performance and how it is to be improved. There are numerous instances of intrinsically-motivated people in music, in the arts and in sport, who are principally concerned with seeking perfection rather than social standing. Indeed, a number frequently shun publicity. With the competence-orientated student social considerations are of secondary importance and the attendant stresses correspondingly reduced. Thus, the student is in a better position to learn from an adverse experience and is less likely to be overwhelmed by failure anxiety or the desire not to 'let people down'.

7. Devaluing the importance of the event

A cognitive strategy which may be effectively employed in some cases is for a person to try to reduce the perceived importance of an examination. This particular approach raises some obvious problems. Teachers whose overriding considerations concern the commitment of their pupils are likely to become alarmed at the thought that it might be in the best interests of some if they were not to try so hard! Again examinations such as A levels and degree examinations are clearly very important to the vast majority of students. However, in the case of able, committed students who continually do well in the practice or mock examinations but underachieve and do relatively badly in the examinations proper, it might well be that in the latter situation they experience adverse stress reactions to the detriment of performance. One explanation for this situation is that students are too highly motivated and overconcerned about the results. Frequently the one major difference between the mock examination on the one hand and the examination proper on the other, is one of importance. There are many examples of this variation in performance occurring between practice sessions and the 'real thing', which are commonplace in sport and other popular activities. Thus, people bat with abandon in the 'nets', they play like Wimbledon champions in the practice 'knock ups' and perform near miracles as practice goalkeepers. Yet when it comes to the actual match, they fail to achieve anything and often do not even play the games competitively. All three of these sports activities have to be performed in highly stressful competitive situations in which it is vital to play well and not make mistakes — certainly in the case of goalkeepers. Even the thought of playing in these situations is enough to deter many people who know in advance that they will do badly because of their fear of performing before large crowds of critical spectators. Earlier reference was made to driving cars, and driving tests provide a daily illustration of how the importance of the occasion can serve to inhibit performance markedly. Learner drivers whose driving may not have attracted much attention previously are often easily recognized when 'on test'; their driving in some instances being hardly distinguishable from that of the beginner. 'Undue hesitancy' and other phrases which appear on the test form are all indicative of the behavioural reactions to stress. Thus, reducing the importance of the contest or examination serves to reduce the stress response and, in the case of the committed yet overanxious individual, to enhance performance.

This approach shows that in some cases it can be beneficial for a student to try to reduce excessive drive. Research generally indicates that test performance can be improved by strategies which do this, one of which is to devalue the importance of the event. It must be emphasized, however, that strategies which reduce anxiety and frustration should be employed only with highly motivated, anxious students; for students who are not particularly anxious or have a low level of motivation, such a strategy is clearly not appropriate and would be more likely to lower performance.

8. Modelling behaviour

Some extremely interesting research has been carried out by Sarason (1972) which shows that the learning and perform-ance of individuals are enhanced when they are given the opportunity of modelling their behaviour on successful performers who are skilled and able to cope with stressful situations. Modelling of behaviour is not uncommon in sport and a number of international players have modelled their play, at least to some extent, on former internationals. Tom Graveney, for example, the Gloucestershire and England batsman was very similar in much of his stroke-play to his former captain, the late Walter Hammond. The opportunity to observe someone working under stress in some problem-solving activity in a positive, constructive way provides the observer with an adaptive model to copy and to imitate for his own future behaviour under similar circumstances. High-anxious people seem to be particularly responsive to demonstrations of how problems can be analysed and approached (Sarason, 1975). There is even value in listening to a successful but anxious perfomer relating how he or she copes with the stress of the situation. In Sarason's work, for example, a coping, anxious model was used who described herself as being high on test anxiety but was able to cope with it by concentrating on the task in hand. Listening to the model's account of how she coped enhanced the performance of high-anxious subjects and indicated their receptiveness and ability to apply information and to adapt their approach to the task successfully.

9. Systematic desensitization procedures

Properly supervised and conducted systematic desensitization is an effective technique which is employed in the management of stress. Some of the research has involved students as subjects who experience 'stage fright' when it comes to public speaking. Following a severe set-back some people may require more than a basic relaxation programme to help them. There are also other individuals who are particularly prone to 'stage fright' and who may be overwhelmed by the sheer intensity of stress created by a public performance. Systematic desensitization has proved to be an effective technique in these cases.

The first step in the desensitization procedure is for the subject to acquire and to experience a feeling of deep relaxation. The relaxation technique which is frequently followed is that of progressive relaxation (Jacobson, 1938) or one of the many modifications of this technique. The next step is to draw up a list or a hierarchy of anxiety-provoking stimuli which are related in some way to the feared situation or object. Since this book is specifically concerned with test anxiety and examination stress it might be appropriate to take a hypothetical case, using examinations as the anxiety-provoking stimulus or situation.

On his own, or with the help of a tutor or counsellor, a student identifies, for example, 20 events or situations which are related to his experience of examinations. These 20 items are then drawn up into a list (Table 1) — number 20 being the item which causes least anxiety, with the listed items then proceeding in turn through those which elicit increasing degrees of anxiety, culminating in item number 1, the examination itself.

80

Table 1 *Hierarchical list of text-anxiety stimuli — hypothetical case*

1. Sitting the examination.
2. Picking up the question paper.
3. Waiting to go into the examination.
4. Travelling to the examination centre.
5. The morning of the examination.
6. The evening before the examination.
7. A week before the examination.
8. A month before the examination.
9. Mock examination — timed.
10. Mock examination — untimed.
11. Reading about examinations in the newspaper.
12. Hearing the word 'examination'.
13. Hearing the word 'test'.
14. Rows of people writing.
15. Textbooks.
16. Desks.
17. Chairs.
18. A4 paper.
19. Pen.
20. Pencil.

The next stage is to achieve a deep state of relaxation. In this relaxed state each item, stress situation or object is visualized in turn, beginning with item number 20 — in this case a pencil — which causes the student the least stress. If, while visualizing the pencil, the student feels relaxed and comfortable with no feelings of anxiety, he then proceeds to visualizing the next item in the hierarchy — in this case a pen — and if he still feels comfortable and at ease he proceeds to visualize item number 18, and so on to item number 1 — sitting the external examination. If the student feels anxious when visualizing a particular item he should stop and try to deepen his state of relaxation before resuming to visualize the item causing anxiety. If anxiety feelings do make it impossible for the student to proceed further in the hieararchy, then it may be necessary to lengthen the programme to include additional items. For example, if the problem arises at item number 4, then three or four additional items can be included which elicit more anxiety than item 5 but less anxiety than item 4.

If the student is able to reach the stage (item 1) where he is able to imagine sitting the examination without feeling anxious, the chances are that this will prove to be the case and that he will be able to take the examination in a comfortable emotional state.

In following this technique the student should try to get as vivid a picture as possible of the item or situation; the ability to achieve this does seem to improve with practice. Research shows that arousal levels, as indicated by heart rate, respiration rate and skin conductance, parallel subjectively reported feelings of anxiety as they are elicited by the visualization of particular situations. Systematic desensitization has been widely used in the treatment of test anxiety. Several research studies show it to be an effective technique. As few as eight one-hour treatment sessions have been reported as being sufficient to bring about a marked decrease in test anxiety in American university students (Tryon, 1980).

The process of acquiring the relaxation response is, as has been said elsewhere, facilitated by biofeedback training which provides an individual with objective evidence of the progress he is making in acquiring this skill. Systematic densensitization methods and techniques are available on audio-cassette tape, and generally this is a very effective medium. Taped instruction includes relaxation instructions and questions about any anxieties which the visualized situations, or stimulus of situations and objects, may evoke. If fear is felt the subject should immediately switch off the recorder and engage in relaxation.

The use of the imagination in visualizing situations which evoke anxiety can be almost as effective as the actual real life experience. Use of the imagination has a number of obvious practical advantages. Situations can be tailored in the imagination to suit the particular needs of individual students and, of course, visualizing is convenient and economical in terms of time. As we have said earlier, repeated experience of situations does not necessarily solve anything. Thus, frequent experience of flying in aeroplanes does not necessarily allay anxiety. Indeed, if the experience is unpleasant it is likely to make things worse. It is necessary to experience a situation which in the past has elicited anxiety and for this to be paired with a state of relaxation. Relaxation has been shown to be incompatible with anxiety. In other words, an individual

has to learn a new association with a situation which elicits
anxiety. Thus, in a state of relaxation the individual is
exposed to situations which elicit anxiety; if the relaxed
response is dominant no anxiety should be experienced.
Wolpe (1969), who was largely responsible for developing
systematic desensitization as a therapeutic measure, argued
that since anxiety reactions are learned they can therefore be
unlearned. The counsellor should explain at the outset that
effective training methods exist but that they require practice.

10. Cognitive modification

Sarason (1975) considers that high test-anxious students
tend to become self-preoccupied and attend to internal events
rather than to the task in hand; he sees such behaviour as mal-
adaptive and serving no useful purpose. This behaviour can,
however, be modified (Sarason, 1972). Self-preoccupation is
characterized by doubt and feelings of inadequacy. Sarason
argues that people can be trained to develop coping skills to
counter self-preoccupations which interfere with performance; training programmes can be developed which will meet
the needs of many groups including those of test-anxious
students. The training programme to develop coping
mechanisms which he outlines, incorporates a multifacted
approach. It includes providing information, modelling,
self-monitoring, attentional training, relaxation and practice,
and reinforcement procedures. It is considered that whether a
person is performing a task or thinking about a problem,
practice together with reward is necessary for shaping
adaptive psychological functioning. Cognitive skills can be
assessed and learning programmes can be developed for the
acquisition of these skills.

Cognitive modification aims to shift the focus of attention from self-preoccupation to task-orientated behaviour,
and at the same time to reduce or eliminate the worry
component of test anxiety. With most test-anxious students
it is frequently necessary to reappraise the situation. People
can select how they choose to interpret circumstances; for
example, if a car breaks down on a journey there are usually
several options open to the driver. He may react negatively
and fret, fume and generally bemoan his fate; alternatively,
he may attempt to locate the fault, to seek assistance or to
find another form of transport. A number of negative and

positive options are open to him. Negative approaches solve nothing whereas positive approaches seek to solve the problem in some way; if one approach fails then another is tried. People are often conditioned and predisposed to respond and behave in certain ways.

With respect to examinations Sarason (1975) considers that test-anxious individuals share negative attitudes and tend to indulge in negative self-talk both before and during the examination. In examination situations they emit personalized, derogatory, self-critical worry responses which disrupt attention and test performance. Thus, a person who engages in negative self-talk is not really concentrating on the paper and is not continually trying to work out how particular questions which present initial difficulty might be answered.

Sarason (1975) suggests various techniques to develop a positive approach and to improve concentration. The use of positive self-talk can be helpful, and in this connection a list of positive statements can be drawn up to suit individual needs. These are then repeated over and over again until they are said almost involuntarily. Some examples of the kind of phrases the author has in mind are:

— 'Now I know how to relax I shall do better.'
— 'I am aiming to pass that examination.'
— 'My attitude is changing for the better.'
— 'I am gaining in confidence every day.'

Unfortunately, however, it is invariably negative statements which anxious examination candidates seem to use. Typical of these are:

— 'I'm hopeless at examinations.'
— 'I know I shall go to pieces.'
— 'I know I shall fail.'
— 'I never have any luck with the questions.'
— 'I don't know why I bother to try.'

Such statements are of no help to any candidate and are described as negative because they are indicative of a person's lack of confidence and only serve further to lower his morale. Self-critical, deprecative comments such as these which disrupt concentration by distracting the student from the actual examination paper should be eliminated entirely and replaced with positive statements which direct attention to the question paper and, therefore, enhance performance.

Cognitive modification involves cognitive reappraisal and it is important that the test-anxious student learns to re-appraise examinations in a positive way. It might be thought that people who appraise problem situations in a positive way are not really facing up to reality and are engaging in wishful thinking. This is not a correct interpretation of this strategy. With a positive approach a person is looking for a solution to the problem while being fully aware of the difficulties. As with the example of the car breakdown discussed earlier, a person with a positive approach is looking for some way to solve the situation rather than just doing nothing.

Cognitive modification, therefore, emphasizes the importance of developing and maintaining a constructive mood and approach to problem situations. This is an effective way of coping with the distractions, self-preoccupation and worrying thoughts about abilities and difficulties which cause tension and stress. Tension, in turn, contributes towards the development of negative attitudes and feelings in similar situations in the future. Thus diagnosis and assessment of a person's thoughts during test performance, if nothing else, does make people aware of such behaviour. Negative self-talk and the images this creates need to be diagnosed as a first step in the treatment of test anxiety. Thus, exposing people to test situations or problem situations provides a means of finding out when, how and why people get distracted. It is also important to gain information concerning the duration of the distraction periods and the way people react to them.

Thus cognitive modification is generally directed towards treating the worry aspect of test anxiety. This involves diagnosis of worry and frequently a reappraisal of situations in order to view these in a more constructive and positive way. Positive self-talk helps while negative self-statements need to be eliminated; again, students can be helped if they are regularly reminded to attend to the task in hand.

The techniques outlined in this chapter can be viewed as coping skills which people can employ in any stressful situation and not just with respect to examinations. Most people can acquire these skills but, as with the learning of any skill, they do require systematic practice over a period of time. This period can be quite short but the actual length depends on the specific needs of individual people. Research investigations show that treatment procedures can be very effective in reducing test anxiety. A daily period of 30 minutes' practice over a three-week period is sufficient for many people to start to see the difference in their ability to cope with stress. The relaxation programme outlined in this chapter is also available in audio-cassette form and it has proved to be most effective in reducing test-anxiety in adults and young people.

There is a considerable amount of evidence that the stress management techniques outlined in this chapter are effective in reducing test anxiety. Preliminary counselling and careful diagnosis are important for people to be made aware of the nature of their response to stress. They need to know how their behaviour is likely to be influenced, both cognitively and emotionally, by examination stress. Counselling is helpful and there are a number of test instruments available which can provide a framework for diagnostic interviews. These tests were described in Chapter 2. Because of the complexity of the condition a multifaceted approach is often needed to effect both a reduction in test anxiety and a corresponding improvement in academic performance.

Much stress is avoidable. Severe, prolonged stress is debilitating and harmful in several ways. Early diagnosis and assessment, therefore, are priorities in the education of the test-anxious student.

Summary

This chapter has examined the nature of stress and some of the sources of stress, particularly as they relate to school and college environments. Reactions to stress have been described as they affect the bodily, emotional, cognitive and behavioural reactions of people generally. The relationship between stress and performance has been discussed with particular reference to test anxiety and examination stress. Finally, a number of techniques and strategies have been outlined which can be effectively employed in the management of stress. It has to be emphasized that problems, and reactions to them, are often highly individualistic and people cannot all be helped and treated in the same way. Diagnosis of problems and the assessment of individual needs are important and these are among the concerns of the chapters which follow.

A number of writers make the valid point that stress is an inevitable part of everyday life. Life, in fact, would be very dull without some stress. Indeed, many stressful activities, in sport and elsewhere for example, are sought after for the interest, excitement and challenges which they bring. However, noxious stimuli which threaten self-esteem can be harmful in several ways, not only to a person's morale but also to his emotional and physical health and general well-being. The main concern of this book is with examination stress which is a major source of worry for students both at sixth form level and at university or college. However, much examination stress is avoidable and can be reduced, in many cases, to relatively mild levels by tackling one of its major sources, uncertainty. The way to do this is by providing the student with as much information as possible. Uncertainty can be reduced still further by adequate emotional and intellectual preparation, which is one of the concerns of some of the later chapters in this book. Where stress continues to remain a problem, effective stress management techniques, such as those outlined earlier in this chapter, may be used to minimize, if not to eliminate, harmful effects. Issues concerning the actual employment of those strategies are explored in later chapters.

However, it seems that there will always be lingering uncertainty for a number of people which results in anxiety and apprehension. Some people find it hard to forget past unfortunate experiences of tests and examinations, and the memory of these is a source of uncertainty, however well prepared they are on future occasions. Following a bad tennis defeat many years ago and before he trained as a psychologist, the author experienced these nagging doubts for several matches afterwards. Apprehension can be present even when there is just an element of risk. Some experiments, for example, have shown that individuals with a ten per cent risk of receiving a shock were more apprehensive and jumpy than individuals with a 50 per cent chance! Perhaps some uncertainty arises out of the element of luck which exists with tests, examinations and competitive events generally. Students can be neither convinced nor certain of the outcome, in spite of knowing that they have the ability and are thoroughly prepared. For example, the author recently overheard a candidate who had just been informed that he had obtained 88 per cent in a mock A level physics paper say to his friend, 'Ah! but that doesn't count'.

Apart from lingering thoughts of past experiences, people may be uncertain and start worrying about how they will feel or what sort of form they will be in on the day. Although intrinsic variability exists with respect to intellectual performance from one occasion to another, as is well known from experience with intelligence testing, individual variations in measured ability over a very short period are generally extremely small and are no real cause for concern. There is also the anxiety which may stem from uncertainty about the questions; there is no doubt that luck is a factor, though not anything like a decisive one, in examinations as it is also in a large number of competitive situations.

In any case it should be borne in mind that a moderate level of anxiety is, of course, helpful and is needed to perform to a high standard. For those who find the time immediately before an examination one of anxious self-preoccupation (they should not if they practise the appropriate stress management techniques sufficiently) the advice of the American philosopher William James could well be helpful:

> 'If you want really to do your best in an examination, fling away the books the day before. Go out and play or go to bed and sleep and I am sure the results next day will encourage you to use the method permanently.'
>
> (Quoted in Maddox, 1963)

The salient point which it is hoped will be emerging from the general line of argument in this chapter, and which will be underlined and emphasized at intervals throughout this book, is that the ability to perform well under pressure is something which can be *learned*. Last minute advice is likely to be of little value. What is needed is the development of effective coping strategies which will enable the individual to remain in control in highly stressful competitive conditions.

Conclusion

The overall objective of a programme designed to reduce test anxiety is for a person to have greater control over certain physiological conditions, over his emotions and over cognitive functioning. The objectives of a stress management/anxiety reduction programme need to be spelt out clearly. This will help the student to monitor progress. People need to understand the nature of their response to stress; in this way they will be better able to appreciate the function of the techniques employed. For test-anxious students typical objectives in a programme designed to reduce test-anxiety would be as follows:

1. The ability to exercise some degree of voluntary control over both anxiety and arousal levels.

2. The ability to shift the focus of attention from self-preoccupied worrying behaviour to externally-directed, task-orientated behaviour, resulting in improved concentration.

3. The development of a positive attitude. This means developing coping skills which are adaptive. An approach should be developed whereby a person is persistently looking for ways in which problems can be solved and difficulties surmounted. In effect a start is made towards tackling problems in a positive way.

4. The ability to perform effectively under pressure. Peak or near peak performances should be consistently achieved.

89

References

Davies, D. E. (1984) 'Maximising Examination Performance'. Audio Programme. Performance Programmes, Malvern.

Eysenck, H. J. and Rachman, S. (1965) *The Causes and Cures of Neurosis.* Routledge and Kegan Paul, London.

Fenz, W. D. and Epstein, S. (1969) Stress in the air. *Psychology Today* 22-8 and 58-9.

Jacobson, E. (1938) *Progressive Relaxation.* The University of Chicago Press, Chicago.

Maddox, H. (1963) *How to Study.* Pan Books, London.

Mandler, G. and Sarason, S. B. (1952) A study of anxiety and learning. *Journal of Abnormal and Social Psychology.* 47, 166-73.

Meichenbaum, D. H. (1972) Cognitive modification of test anxious college students. *Journal of Consulting and Clinical Psychology.* 39, 370-80.

Sarason, I. G. (1972) Experimental approaches to test anxiety. Attention and uses of information. In Spielberger, C. D. (ed.) *Anxiety. Current trends in theory and research, 2.* Academic Press, New York.

Sarason, I. G. (1975) Anxiety and self-preoccupation. In Sarason, I. G. and Spielberger, C. D. (eds) *Stress and Anxiety, 2.* Hemisphere/ Widey, New York.

Tryon, G. S. (1980) The measurement and treatment of test anxiety. *Review of Educational Research.* 50 (2), 343-72.

Welford, A. T. (1967) *Fundamentals of Skill.* Methuen, London.

Wolpe, J. (1969) *The Practice of Behavioural Therapy.* Pergammon, New York.

Zajoric (1965) Social Facilitation. *Science.* 149-274.

Chapter 4

Fatigue, Worry, Health and Learning

Introduction

A survey conducted by the author (Davies, 1986) revealed that a substantial proportion of A level students experienced stress-related problems both in the months preceding the examination and during the examination itself, to the almost certain detriment of performance. Forty-four per cent of students, for example, reported that they worried during the examination. Even more (69.7 per cent) 'worried a lot' in the weeks and months before the examination. Some 60.5 per cent of students considered that worry had an adverse effect of their health. Minor health problems included sleeping difficulties (33.8 per cent) and loss of energy (26.7 per cent). The survey showed that only 20.3 per cent received any help and training in stress management and in reducing worry.

Sleep and fatigue

Sleep is essential for health and vitality. It is during sleep that energy is restored. It is the quality of sleep which is important rather than the duration. For effective performance adequate sleep is essential — the test is simply how a person feels. Loss of sleep occurring over a few days is not harmful. Oswald and Adam (1983), for example, consider that some students who study late at night in the week may suffer from acute fatigue but are able to recover when they sleep for periods of up to 14 hours at the weekend. Chronic fatigue, on the other hand, is harmful and occurs as the result of loss of rest and sleep over an extended period of time. Chronic fatigue results in poor general health, loss of energy, low vitality and lowered concentration, as is discussed more fully in Chapter 6.

People become nervous and irritable and have little per-severance. Loss of sleep over a period of weeks or months is followed by a marked fall in efficiency and a lowering of the general capacity for work. Of those students with sleeping difficulties in the author's survey 50 per cent also had concentration problems, 40 per cent felt tired and 27 per cent felt excessively nervous during the examination. It seems certain that adequate rest and sleep are essential for performance to be consistently efficient.

The quality and duration of sleep can be improved in several ways. Oswald and Adam in their book *Get a Better Night's Sleep* argue that it is important for people to persist with regular times for going to bed and for getting up. A regular routine, they argue, helps to strengthen the 'biological clock', the biorhythm which works on a 24-hour cycle. People with irregular sleep patterns have been found to have less sense of well-being, to feel low throughout the day, and to be less efficient than people who go to bed at the same time each night and rise at the same time each morning.

Better sleep can also be achieved by taking regular daily exercise. It has been found that people who exercise frequently not only fall asleep more quickly but the quality of their sleep is generally better than that of people who do not exercise. The emphasis is on moderate but regular exercise.

The quality of sleep can be improved by reducing tension and worry. Sleep is closely related to daytime experiences and feelings. People who are anxious and worried have relatively poor sleep compared to those individuals who are content and well adjusted socially. Worry is a major reason why people not only take a long time to go to sleep but when they do so the quality of their sleep is poor. Thus for better sleep worries need to be minimized or, ideally, resolved. The problem of worry is discussed in the next section and ways in which the worried student can be helped are outlined.

Worry

Worry is a serious problem for students both in relation to their health and also to their performance in examinations. The author's survey of 221 students showed that a large proportion 'worry a lot' before an examination. In many cases students begin to worry months before the actual examination as is indicated in Table 2.

Table 2 *Pre-examination worry*

Stage at which students begin to worry	%
12 months before	1.4
6 months before	7.0
3 months before	13.3
1 month before	32.3
1 week before	17.0

Students who were worrying a lot before the examination considered that this had an adverse effect upon their health. They reported that they suffered from a variety of minor health problems; these are indicated in Table 3.

Table 3 *Pre-examination worry and health problems of students*

	%
Sleeping difficulties	33.8
Loss of energy/feeling tired	26.7
Headaches	18.3
Lack of appetite	12.0
Stomach upsets	11.9

13.3 per cent of students suffered from three or more of the health problems listed and 13 per cent from two.

A substantial proportion of students (44 per cent) reported that they worried during the actual examination. The main worries are listed in Table 4.

Table 4 *Examination worries of students*

	%
Letting people down	19.7
Past failures	19.7
Other students being better	11.2
Having no luck	6.0
What other people might think	4.0

The cumulative effects of prolonged worry and chronic fatigue had an adverse effect on the examination performance of a substantial proportion of students. More than a fifth considered that their concentration was poor and nearly as many were excessively nervous; 4.2 per cent either fainted or experienced dizziness. Just over half the students suffered from panic reactions during the examination. These included switching to and fro from one question to another (35.9 per cent) and continual checking and re-checking of work (25.3 per cent).

Minimizing worry

Thus it is clearly important to minimize worry. Although, as the survey indicates, there are worries which are common to large numbers of students, worry is often a highly individual matter — what may worry one student can leave another unconcerned. Thus the first step in minimizing worry is a diagnosis which will reveal what it is that people are worrying about. Some of the chief worries which students have concerning examination performance are listed below:

- Letting people down, eg parents and teachers
- Past failures
- Other students being better
- Luck
- What other people might think/loss of prestige
- Unfamiliar surroundings/intimidating prospect of large examination hall
- Being a poor examinee
- Health/poor sleep
- Uncertainty concerning progress
- Uncertainty about what is expected
- Dislike of subject
- Feelings of inadequacy/low self-esteem.

Some sources of worry

Uncertainty, low self-esteem, feelings of inadequacy and fear of failure are all sources of worry.

Failure to do well can be demoralizing as students fail to gain the reinforcement which comes with success. Some students may begin to worry that they are letting people down and as a result become overanxious and overactivated before and during competitive situations. Failure, over a series of tests and examinations, can lead to a serious loss of confidence. Adverse criticism in this instance is

94

likely further to discourage a student who is already doing badly. The failing student expects criticism and hence this merely serves to confirm his beliefs. In a number of cases students develop negative self-concepts and, not unnaturally, begin to feel apprehensive in learning situations, particularly where their performance is being judged or evaluated. Pessimistic attitudes must be avoided as a student's self-concept, that is the expectations he has of himself, will not only be influenced by his performance in examinations, but also by the expectations of teachers and parents, and by the way they behave towards him. Where a student values the opinions of the teacher he will tend to internalize what the teacher thinks about him and he will, in time, begin to perform in his work to confirm those expectations and beliefs. For example, if a student gains the impression that the people responsible for his education do not consider him to be a good examinee, there will be a strong tendency to fulfil this prophecy with a student coming to believe that he has, in fact, a poor temperament for examinations. A teacher's expectation of performance, therefore, is generally a powerful factor determining performance levels; there is much research in the educational field concerning the influence which the expectations of 'significant others' have on a person's own motivation and expectations. By significant others is meant the people who are regarded by the student as being important and having credibility. Thus, it has been seen that an optimistic approach by the teacher tends to arouse higher motivational levels and expectations in the student, and a pessimistic approach to result in a lowering of motivational levels and of expectations.

Almost inevitably, the majority of people are subjected to a variety of stresses, both at school and later at college, which can create serious problems for some. Cohen (1972), for example, found in his survey of first year college of education students that high-anxious students reported a greater number of problems than did low-anxious students. These problems were concerned with personal and social relationships, with health and with worries concerning the general approach to work at college level. Predictably, difficulty in adjusting to change in learning and teaching styles was also found to be a source of anxiety by Wankowski (1973). The greater emphasis on independent study was found to pose problems for many, but in particular for over-anxious students who, when at school, had relatively closer teacher guidance and support. At college level Wankowski considers that anxiety in students can be reduced by teaching situations which are highly structured and predictable. Wankowski recommends smaller classes, frequent tutor-student contact and counselling concerning study difficulties. Wankowski considers that course objectives generally need to be spelt out much more clearly than is frequently the case. He finds that students can be in doubt concerning their progress through infrequent feedback.

Fostering self-esteem

What needs to be provided is a learning environment which will enhance rather than damage a person's self-concept. Much can be done to reduce worry associated with learning by giving a person work with which he is able to cope. In this respect frequent short tests are considerably preferable to the placing of great emphasis on one major examination. Thus, short tasks with a high reward content are needed, as is the case with programmed instruction. Group discussions are helpful as students can share and discuss their work and in this way they may derive some degree of comfort from the knowledge that they are not the only ones with problems and that, in fact, there are many students who have problems, to varying degrees, concerning examinations.

Initially, the student with a poor self-concept needs to be functioning in learning situations in which success is virtually guaranteed. He has a very low tolerance for failure and competitive situations can be disastrous. Worried students need the assurance that they are only competing against their own past performance. In this way they will feel much more secure and will be encouraged to learn. Every opportunity should be taken to enhance feelings of personal accomplishment and to encourage intrinsic motivation.

Modes of instruction

Introduction
Generally, a direct teaching approach with clearly defined objectives is preferable to open-ended and discovery methods

in the case of the student with a poor self-concept. Open-ended and discovery methods create uncertainty, and therefore anxiety, and generally, worried people are unable to respond to the challenge presented by such situations. Insecure people prefer a regular, well-planned, consistent, predictable routine. Any uncertainty concerning what is required of the student must be minimal. It is essential that he has a very clear idea about what he is being asked to do. Birney (1972), in a review of modes of presentation of materials, considers the position of the anxious student in traditional teaching situations. Birney argues that the anxious student will be at a considerable disadvantage in situations which are 'unfamiliar, speeded and threatening'.

Programmed learning

Programmed learning or automatic teaching is in several respects particularly suited to the anxious student. With programmes of the linear type the subject matter is broken down into a series of discrete steps. These are arranged in logical sequence. The extensive development of the linear-type programme has been largely the result of the work of Skinner (1953). A linear programme consists of a series of small frames, each consisting of about two sentences followed by a question. This constructed-response type programme involves the student replying with a short answer to each frame as distinct from the multiple choice programme in which a student selects one answer from a number of possible answers.

Programmed learning has a number of psychological advantages to recommend it. Feedback or knowledge of results is virtually immediate. The student knows straight-away whether he is right or wrong and, therefore, if he is right his response is immediately reinforced. On the other hand, if he is wrong he is able to correct a misunderstanding at once. Further, the programmes are generally so carefully graded that a student is often right 90 per cent of the time so that his learning is being continually rewarded or reinforced. This is highly motivating for the learner. Another advantage of programmed learning, and particularly for the worried student, is that people can work at their own pace. The student is completely independent of others and, therefore, there is not the pressure of having to keep up with the class

97

as a whole. For the anxious student there is the further advantage that shortcomings and mistakes are not publicly exposed and he is not called upon to answer questions in class, as is often the case with more traditional methods of teaching. Programmed learning, since it constantly requires responses from the student, means that the learner is actively involved and is not following a passive role of merely listening to the teacher.

Linear programmes, since they are so carefully graded, generally contain a considerable amount of repetition. They do not, therefore, always present a sufficient challenge for very able and confident students. However, for the anxious, failing student programmed learning of the linear type represents an excellent form of instruction with its high reward content and the fact that students are able to work in private and at their own pace.

Thus programmed learning with its gradual progression, small, carefully graded steps, clear directions and high reward content, gives a sense of security to the anxious student. Feedback is a critical factor in the learning and performance of the anxious student who has a low tolerance for delayed feedback. The worried student, in other words, is very anxious about his progress and the immediate feedback which is a feature of programmed learning gives the student a sense of security and also provides him with frequent experiences of success. Thus programmed instruction, in several respects, would appear to be a particularly appropriate approach for the anxious student. It is an effective mode of instruction in the case of the student with feelings of inadequacy, since the interfering effects on achievement of competitive stress are minimal. Programmed instruction provides a situation which is less threatening than traditional forms of teaching and it provides a framework for learning in which there is little fear of negative evaluation by others. It is a highly structured medium of instruction with very clear explicit directions which minimize uncertainty and, therefore, worry. Additionally, the concrete nature of the materials and the high reward content of the linear type programmes are strongly motivating for students with poor self-concepts.

The Open University places considerable emphasis on

highly structured individualized study. Workbooks are supplied to students in which the objectives of the course are explicitly outlined stage by stage. This is to enable the student to proceed through the work on his own, although tutors are available for consultation if needed. The import-ance of group work and discussion varies from course to course, but the course materials contain booklists and course workbooks containing carefully graded exercises and activities to enable the student to work on his own. Intermediate tests enable the student to check his own progress which can be highly motivating. Open University students, many with considerable personal prestige at stake and in responsible jobs, are studying under considerable pressure and require this highly structured approach to study for the benefit of their own emotional health. Additionally, students may be supplied with audio-cassette tapes, visual aids and also, where relevant, test materials. At the Open University centres booths are available for students to work in private. In this situation, the risk of any negative evaluation by tutors and peers is minimal. With this highly structured approach which has clearly defined goals and regular feedback, motivation is generally high and the whole learning environment provides the student with a sense of security since there is little uncertainty for the student. As with programmed instruction the student is able to work unhindered at his own pace. This approach is also good for morale since the student is made to feel responsible for his work and the improvement he makes. Traditional approaches to learning contain more uncertainty and threat, and in this sense are not always appropriate for students with poor self-concepts.

Students who are worried may have ineffective study habits. The value of effective study habits is underlined in an excellent book by Maddox called *How to Study*. The value and importance of study skills is often a neglected area in student education. Maddox details a number of important study skills. These include planning objectives, daily records, and personal timetables, and also the use of the library, note-taking, reading, essay writing and examination technique. Maddox discusses issues such as fatigue and health, and points to the value of well-planned, distributed study and the need for rest and recreation. For the confused and worried student this is an essential handbook.

Concern about such matters as past failures, letting people down, other students being better, etc, serve to underline the emotional problems which many students face. Consequently, the traditional approach in education, concentrating as it does almost exclusively on academic study and development, is too narrowly based and inadequate for the preparation needs of a substantial proportion of the school population. What is required is a wider, more sustained, systematic approach which aims to minimize worry and and is concerned with both the physical and the emotional health and development of the individual.

References

Birney, R. C. et al. (1969) *Fear of Failure*. Van Norstrand Reinhold, New York.

Cohen, L. (1972) Personality and changing problems among first year College of Education students. *Durham Research Review*. 28, Spring, 617-22.

Davies, D. E. (1986) *Examination performance: a survey of the stress-related problems of A level students*. Unpublished survey.

Maddox, H. (1963) *How to Study*. Pan Books, London.

Oswald, I. and Adam, K. (1983) *Get a Better Night's Sleep*. Martin Dunitz, London.

Skinner, B. F. (1953) *Science and Human Behaviour*. Macmillan, New York.

Skinner, B. F. (1968) *The Technology of Teaching*. Appleton-Century Crofts, New York.

Wankowski, J. A. (1973) *Temperature, nutrition and academic achievement*. University of Birmingham Educational Survey.

Chapter 5

Psychological Preparation for Examinations

The concept of psychological preparation

The various motivational and emotional problems which can beset students lend credence to the argument that just as an extended period is devoted to intellectual or academic preparation, so too should some time be spent in developing the emotional capacities of the student. The principal concern of psychological preparation is that the student will learn how to cope with stress situations to the extent that he is able to do reasonable justice to his ability and commitment. Psychological preparation is seen as incorporating a sustained systematic approach to an attainable standard of performance. The aim is to develop the intellectual and emotional capacities of people to the extent that they have both the ability and the confidence to deal with the many pressures which are an inherent feature of competitive examinations. A whole variety of strategies is available which can be developed to suit the needs of individual students, to help them to become increasingly psychologically 'tough' or resilient and at the same time to cultivate a positive, thrusting approach to the examination situation.

The need for psychological preparation

The problem for many students is that they simply do not have any kind of system for study. This means that they have little idea of goals, progress or study methods. Beard and Sinclair (1980) cite 'study difficulties' as one of the main factors in student withdrawal and failure. Students complained about lack of guidance, lack of help with study methods and uncertainties concerning the purpose of the course. Beard and Sinclair consider that it is the student's experiences in the first year at university which largely determine whether they withdraw, fail or succeed. Vagueness concerning both short- and long-term goals is often a factor. Wankowski (1973), for example, found that poorly defined goal orientations were a factor in examination failure. In the Birmingham investigations well over half the students seeking counselling had only vaguely defined study goals. Investigations undertaken in Australia by Kearney (1969) and Pentony (1968) underline the need to have well-defined goals for academic success. Both Kearney and Pentony found that students with study problems had little sense of direction and a general uncertainty, and indeed ignorance, concerning their goals and the purpose of the courses they were following. A problem which arises in the absence of clearly defined goals is that students have little idea of what is expected of them. Beard and Sinclair, for example, found that a major source of worry and dissatisfaction among students is that they have difficulty in discovering the precise, overall purpose of the courses they are following. The absence of clearly defined goals and objectives leads to a variety of problems. Students find that they are often unable to manage their time and feel that they are working in a vacuum with little idea of where they are going and how far they have progressed. Such a situation is clouded with uncertainty and worry — particularly concerning their progress in relation to that of other students.

Goal setting

The probable importance of having clearly defined goals has been demonstrated by Gaa (1971). Gaa found that students who attended weekly goal-setting meetings not only achieved higher test scores than a control group but also developed more positive attitudes towards the course. Gaa considers that the data from his findings may be interpreted to mean that goal setting was a factor in enhancing the intrinsic motivation of the students.

Left to their own devices few students, it seems, spend much effort on any kind of systematic planning. This means that without concrete goals, especially in the short term, students will experience some difficulty in assessing their progress. Further, if the course of study has not been broken down into a series of sub-goals, the likelihood is that students will not have any particularly clear perceptions regarding the amount of work involved in meeting the standards and demands of the examination. This means that students who underestimate the difficulty of the task may leave insufficient time for study. Others who overestimate the difficulty may become anxious and begin to worry about their feelings of inadequacy. Finally, if goals are not actually written down then students must rely on their memories, which may not be particularly reliable.

Short-term goals, embedded into a long-term study pro-gramme, are important in that they provide people with a sense of achievement. This helps in the development of positive attitudes towards work and it is an excellent strategy for the development of self-confidence. Nothing succeeds like success.

Study difficulties

Poore and Pappas (1974) suggest that student problems frequently arise through ineffective study skills. Thus, problems can arise when students embark on new courses and begin at new institutions which place a much greater emphasis on independent study with, in some cases, the mini-mum of teacher contact time. Problems can even arise with such details as notetaking and how to use the library. Major concerns such as time management and self-evaluation of course work are very important and need to be incorporated into a study programme at an early stage. Maddox (1963) estimates that in schools, for every two hours spent in the classroom students are expected to spend one hour in private study. In contrast, for a similar period of tutor-contact time college students would be expected to spend four times the amount of time in private study that the schoolboy is expected to do, ie four hours. If anything, Maddox seems to be underestimating the amount of time students in higher education should be spending in private study relative to classroom work. At school there are set hours for private study. At college and university this is not the case and deciding when to study and for how long is plainly the responsibility of the student. Thus the student is faced with making decisions and choices in this respect. Further, the

actice in school is for set work to be handed in at
class meeting or within a fairly short period.
llege, the practice is to have fewer but larger assign-
which can be submitted on a half-term vacation or
wh.. : year basis. Thus, the whole emphasis on independent
study places much more responsibility on the student than
is generally the case in schools and students can have problems concerning time management and adjusting to a wholly
different approach to work and study. With these considerations in mind it can be argued that all students, and not
just those who say they have difficulties, should receive
conselling in time management and study skills. Research by
Sarason (1978) shows that test-anxious students who received
training and study counselling showed significant gains in
their academic performance.

Test anxiety

Test anxiety is a major problem for a large number of
students. Unfortunately for the overanxious student, the
official view is often that test anxiety is inevitable, that examinations are part of college life and, therefore, responsible
students are expected to be able to cope with the problems
which may arise. In general, a high level of anxiety depresses
performance and, in the extreme case, can thoroughly disrupt performance to the extent that the individual becomes
incapable of making any kind of response at all. Test-anxious
students are likely to experience feelings of tension and
apprehension. It is also probable that they will have concentration problems which arise from self-centred worry
cognitions concerning the social consequences of failure.
Furthermore, it is likely that they will be overaroused and
overexcited.

Test-anxious students tend to have poor study habits
(Desiderato and Koshinen, 1969; Wittmeier, 1972) and, in
fact, devote less time to study than do students of a more
stable disposition. The reason for this is that the test-anxious
student tends to spend his time worrying about studying
rather than studying! Time and energy are wasted in worrying
about what to study and ruminating over shortcomings,
difficulties, inadequacies and the social consequences of
failure.

The fact that test anxiety is a major difficulty besetting

106

many students is indicated by the considerable amount of research which has been devoted to diagnosis and treatment. Tryon (1980) alone reviewed 85 investigations dealing with various treatments of test anxiety. Clearly there is a need for psychological preparation for the test-anxious student, both with regard to reducing anxiety and improving study habits and skills.

Training procedures and routines which reduce anxiety are beneficial for the student if they serve to reduce or even to eliminate the time which students spend worrying. Students are, therefore, able to make more efficient use of their time. Dansereau et al. (1979), for example, argue that many students in the pre-examination periods experience a variety of negative emotions including anger, guilt, anxiety and frustration. Such feelings, and the accompanying negative self-talk, serve to distract the student's attention from the task at hand when studying, but much more so in stress situations such as tests and examinations.

From a psychological perspective the idea of planning a study programme has important implications for both teacher and student. Despite the fact that this is probably the most important facet of teaching, it is often the one which is most neglected. This is evident from the work of Beard and Sinclair. There may be little communication, for example, between tutor and student. The term can begin with a student having little understanding of the situation and of the tutor's goals and expectations. It is also possible that he has only rather vague ideas of his own goals and expectations. It is useful to think of a forthcoming course of study in the following three ways:

1. Areas of concern for the student.
2. What specific goals and sub-goals can be set in the areas of concern identified in (1.) above.
3. The ways in which the goals in (2.) above will be set and the strategies which will be employed.

If the tutor's goals are incompatible with those of the student then the beginning of term or, better still, before the beginning of term is the best time to discuss such a problem and find a solution. Ideally, tutor and student should work in harmony and plan a programme for the term or academic year which is mutually acceptable. The sub-goals or intermediate goals and the accompanying tests embedded in the preparation programme should be seen in some kind of hierarchical order in terms of their difficulty, both in a technical or academic sense and also in a fuller psychological sense. It is important for the student to see the whole purpose of these intermediate tests in the perspective of a half-term plan of preparation. It is very important even at this early stage of psychological preparation to state goals in specific, reasonable, behavioural terms. The tutor must push the student to set meaningful, realistic goals — an aspect of teaching that requires considerable insight both into the nature of the subject and the personality and ability of the student.

The final stage in the long-term psychological preparation is actually making the plans work. Here the teacher's role is to encourage behaviour which is consistent with the goals that have been established. During this final stage a periodic review of the stated goals and strategies enables the tutor to provide feedback to the student. The review can be a source of reinforcement or an opportunity to focus attention on the reasons for failure and possibly to adjust goals. Psychological preparation involving the setting up of a systematic, mutually-agreed programme of study between teacher and student has several advantages over a more haphazard approach to study:

1. Clarified goals help the student to see the purpose and direction of the year, and thus to appreciate both what he has to do and what is expected of him.
2. Long-term motivation is enhanced.
3. The student's self-confidence will be improved.
4. Problem behaviour will be reduced or eliminated.
5. There will be increased 'rapport' between tutor and student.

The functions of practice tests

1. Progress

Practice tests provide a means whereby progress towards a final goal can be facilitated. Thus, having established sub-goals or intermediate goals in a study programme, periodic testing becomes necessary to ascertain whether these sub-goals have been achieved. The tests need only be short with much of the preparation consisting of answering one question. It might be thought that students would regard the prospect of periodic testing with alarm and perhaps resentment. However, this is not likely to be the case. Beard and Sinclair (1980) point out, for example, that assessment of work is valued by the great majority of students. When this assessment is both designed and perceived to be helping students it is generally welcomed. The perceived role of the teacher is an important factor and, where the teacher is seen as occupying a teaching role rather than a judgemental one, assessment of work is highly valued. Furthermore, in the particular context of test situations the creation of a competitive situation between students is not envisaged. The only competitive situation which could operate is for a student to compete against himself — that is to try to improve on his own past performances. Most people find competition of the intra variety highly motivating. The author had firsthand experience of this many years ago when working with less able children who had reading difficulties. Following a few counselling sessions the children began to make what was for them fairly rapid progress. This meant that almost daily there were cries of 'Can I do the test? Can I do the test?'

Although students are naturally inclined to be mainly concerned with their grade, a major function of practice tests is the important diagnostic aid which the evaluations provide both for student and teacher. It is in the light of this information that study programmes can be reviewed, if necessary, to meet the changing needs of students. Evaluations are important in that they help to clear a lot of the uncertainty and doubt for the student concerning his progress, and thus avoid a lot of unnecessary anxiety.

2. Evaluation and knowledge of results

Another function of practice tests is that they provide the learner with knowledge of his progress. As was emphasized in Chapter 1, knowledge of results not only acts as a powerful incentive to continue to study, it also provides the individual with valuable information concerning his strengths and weaknesses in a particular subject. Regular and frequent assessment of work, even if the tests are only short, gives the student a relatively clear idea of whether he is doing sufficient work and whether he is on the right lines. Relying largely on end of term tests or one single large-scale, mock examination could well mean that students are in doubt concerning the effectiveness of their study, work methods and progress. Frequent assessment makes students better able to pace their efforts in relation to the tasks still to be accomplished. They have a better idea of how much work still remains to be done and this knowledge helps to avoid unncessary and fatiguing 'cramming' sessions towards the end of term. Tests, even if they 'don't count' are likely to mean that students will be studying and revising in between. Thus cramming is less likely. Evaluations of tests can be a valuable source of information for both teacher and tutor in several important respects. Apart from providing information concerning the technical or academic merits of the scripts, evaluations and assessments can embrace such concerns as decision making, time management, anxiety management, attitudes and concentration, questionnaires, checklists and post-test counselling sessions. Evaluations of tests also enable the student to monitor his own performance; in the light of variations in study methods he begins to get a clearer picture of what works and what does not. Information arising from the evaluations, for example, enables the student to make more intelligent decisions concerning the pacing of study and the setting up of realistic intermediate goals. On the basis of this information, learning strategies can be developed which best meet the needs of individual students. Thus, for a student experiencing test anxiety problems an affective learning strategy might be considered helpful. An example of an affective learning strategy is self-initiated relaxation (SIR).

The diagnostic information which arises from test evaluations can also be very valuable for the teacher. Evaluations can provide information on the strengths and weaknesses of individual students. They also provide information concerning the effectiveness of particular teaching techniques, methods and materials. Evaluations indicate to the teacher how well he is communicating to the student and whether, for example, he is taking into full account the student's ability and experience of the subject. As far as the student is concerned the diagnostic information arising from evaluations of test performances enables the teacher to pin-point areas of difficulty and matters which may require further clarification

and emphasis in future course work. Evaluations, therefore, are particularly valuable in the diagnosis of learning
difficulties.

3. Counselling

It must be remembered at the outset that even the most
sophisticated psychological techniques and strategies in
training are likely to be of little value unless the student sees
them as being directed towards producing the best possible
performance on the occasion of the examination. This is the
case in all situations where people are striving to pass an
examination, to gain some qualification or, for example, to
become an international sportsman. A few years ago the
author was present at the beginning of a 'pressure' tennis
training session when the player — now a member of the
British Davis Cup team — was at odds with the coach over the
need to engage in a particular training activity. He clearly did
not see the point of the activity. This situation can arise and
what may be obvious to the coach, teacher or psychologist
may not be quite so obvious to the student or budding
international athlete. This is particularly likely to be the case
with some of the psychological strategies which may be
employed both in regard to stress reduction and motivational
concerns. Thus it is important to let the student have a very
clear picture of the specific ways in which he will benefit by
following certain routines. It may be sufficient to say that all
the experts do these things, but a clear explanation helps
to clarify points for the student and here, of course, any
theoretical discussion is generally underlined with appropriate
concrete illustrations.

4. Learning experience

Practice tests constitute a significant learning experience.
They require the student to organize material, to marshal
facts and to clarify concepts. Tests give the student experience in the presentation of balanced, reasoned and supported
argument; of distinguishing the salient, the central, features
of a problem. Answering test questions gives the student not
only the opportunity to organize knowledge, but to apply it.
Regular testing enables the student to become thoroughly
conversant with the subject and for the material to be overlearned; it influences an individual's whole approach and

111

attitude to study. The ability to outline and present subject matter in a clear way needs practice. Tests afford an opportunity of acquiring these skills under pressure. In several ways, therefore, tests, even though they may be of short duration, constitute a significant learning experience.

5. Decision making

Practice tests of this kind provide the student with experience of appraising papers and of decision making with respect to question selection. Decision making is a skill and an area in which people need some practice. Some students, for example, take far too long in arriving at a decision and they do not always select the questions covering the topics which they know best.

The problem with making difficult decisions is that the pros and cons are not present in the mind at the same time. Sometimes a particular advantage prevails only to be replaced by a particular disadvantage, perhaps to be followed by an alternative advantage. Thus in everyday life we are constantly faced with making decisions which are not obviously clear cut; people may prevaricate about moving house, changing jobs, how to travel etc. For everyday decisions and for facilitating question selection in tests and examinations, some kind of effective decision-making strategy is required. Examinations involve making several important decisions, such as question selection and the setting of various time-limits.

It is, therefore, a good idea to have a checklist of items on which the pros and cons of answering particular questions can be listed; this is likely to be far more accurate than the immediate response which arises from a superficial glance at the question. This can occur when students make false assumptions concerning expected questions. A checklist might include items concerned with comprehension, knowledge, material, interest and previous experience of similar questions. Table 5 is an example of such a checklist. Ideally, of course, the checklist could be extended in the light of the student's experience of tests. The checklist device can be a means of handling very complex decisions. President Carter, for example, arrived at a decision concerning the B.1 bomber by a strategy of this kind, although involving highly sophisticated analysis.

112

Table 5 *A checklist for deciding on an examination question*

Checklist	Yes	No
1. Do I fully understand the question and any accompanying riders to it?		
2. Do I have sufficient material for an adequate answer?		
3. Is the question a straightforward one?		
4. Have I a clear idea of how to tackle the question?		
5. Have I answered the question or a similar one before?		
6. Does the question interest me?		
7. Do I have a clear idea of what it is that the examiner is asking?		

Students should set aside a certain amount of time for decision making for each question and the checklist procedure should be followed in every case even though initially the choice of a particular question appears to be a straightforward matter. It does happen that people embark on a particular question and then find later on, for one reason or another, that they cannot give an adequate answer. This situation arises sometimes when the question has been misread. Valuable time and energy can be lost in this way for the student is then faced with one, perhaps two, further decisions: he has to decide whether to continue with the question or whether to abandon it. If he makes the latter decision he is then faced with making a decision concerning an alternative question to answer. Much time can be wasted and this is the sort of stress-provoking situation which is best avoided. Maddox in his book *How to Study* suggests that students do make errors of this kind and the author has met several such cases with final degree scripts.

Regular rehearsal of the checklist procedure during practice tests should mean that questions will receive careful preliminary study and that the risk of students starting to write straightaway as many do (Maddox, 1963) will be accordingly reduced. Use of the checklist should serve also to encourage task-orientated behaviour and to enhance concentration.

113

With papers in which there is a choice, the obvious policy is to begin by selecting a question to which you feel you can give a reasonably competent answer. This is important with respect to developing confidence for the paper as a whole.

Time-management also involves allowing adequate time for each question. It is very important that all the questions are answered so a certain amount of time should be allocated for each one. Writing at excessive length on one or two questions will not compensate for failing to make a response to others. If you do start to run out of time then unfinished answers are better than no answers at all.

Concentration

Practice tests also provide an opportunity to investigate a student's ability to concentrate on a test question. A common complaint among students is that they find themselves unable to concentrate during an examination. For one reason or another they sometimes find their minds wandering and they may engage in negative self-talk and even start to day-dream rather than attending to the work in hand. Post-test evaluations and diagnosis counselling serve, if nothing else, to make people aware of such problems. Thus an important purpose of test diagnosis is to find out when, how and why people become distracted. Post-test discussions should also seek to analyse the duration of the distraction periods and a student's reactions to these distractions. Dansereau, et al. (1979), argue that many students, in the run up to the examination or in the pre-evaluation period, experience a variety of negative emotions including anger, guilt, anxiety and frustration. Such feelings and the associated negative self-talk serve to distract the student's attention from the task in hand during study, but this is particularly the case in stress situations such as tests and examinations.

Thus it is important that problems concerning attention and concentration are reviewed and analysed in the post-test period. The tutor or counsellor can discuss problems with the student, and a useful diagnostic instrument which can be used in such a situation is the Cognitive Interference Questionnaire (Sarason, 1978). This particular test seeks to discover the irrelevant thoughts which may preoccupy the student during a test-evaluative situation. The test consists of items which ask the students what they were thinking about during the test or examination and while they were working on particular questions. The student is asked to indicate on a five-point scale ranging from 'never' to 'very often', how frequently each thought occurred to him. Samples of the 'thoughts' are:

— 'I wondered what the examiner would think of me.'

— 'I thought about the difficulty of the problem.'

— 'I thought about how poorly I was doing.'

Students are also asked to indicate the degree to which they felt their mind wandered during the test with respect to particular questions.

The aim of the diagnosis is to find out which external and internal distractions were present. Examples of external distractions might be noises from another room, the movements of the invigilator, the temperature of the room, rustling of papers, etc. Internal distractions might be thoughts or cognitions about doing badly.

It is important in the test situation to maintain a constructive attitude and approach and to be able to learn to cope with external and internal distractions. Distractions can cause considerable tension. Tension in tests may lead to negative attitudes in similar situations in the future. Thus evaluations serve to diagnose and pin-point the source of the difficulties, and to encourage the development of effective positive coping attitudes.

Practice tests also afford an opportunity to study, observe and evaluate how students work under pressure. A useful way of doing this is by a checklist; this helps a teacher to diagnose a student's shortcomings and to work out, with the student, ways in which these shortcomings might be overcome. Use of a checklist enables the teacher to pin-point both satisfactory behaviour and relatively weak points; it provides a systematic means for the observation of behaviour. The checklist can provide a framework for the observation of student performance. Each student is unique and, therefore, a highly individualistic approach to his needs and problems is generally necessary.

Practice tests also provide a means of developing the emotional capacities of the student. The types of stresses which are experienced by students under examination conditions can be simulated during practice tests. A programme of preparation can be established which initially would include a series of short lower level tests providing the student with the opportunity to develop his own coping mechanisms and to start to accommodate to stress and learn how to handle it. This is a far better form of preparation than the 'one off' mock examination which is often viewed as a dress rehearsal for the real thing. The idea is to simulate, but in a gradual manner, the types of stresses in practice tests which the student experiences in the examination situation proper. Emotional preparation is important if a student is to bring his feelings under control. Students must not be pushed beyond the level of their emotional maturity. Examination performance is dependent, at least to some extent, on the ability to cope with the perceived stress of the situation. The pressures in practice test situations can be increased in a variety of ways. One way is to reduce the time limit, another is to provide incentives of various kinds.

Preparing for examinations: some general considerations

There are some common elements in preparing students for examinations:

1. The student must be appropriately motivated for the examination. This is a complex area which is dealt with elsewhere in the book. The major purpose of motivation is to stimulate the student to perform at his best in the particular examination. Therefore, an examination must be seen in the context of the long-term development of the student and not necessarily as the ultimate test of ability. It is because of individual differences among students that the use of personal private comment to stimulate or relax can be, where appropriate, very important. This can only be achieved if the tutor knows in detail how each student in his charge thinks and operates in a stressful situation. Once again, the best way for the tutor to develop this awareness of individual reactions is for him to simulate those types of stresses in practice which are experienced in

an exam situation. Another alternative is to use a series of lower level tests as part of the build-up to the major examination and in this way to develop the coping strategy of the student.

2. The appropriate attitude needs to be developed. Obviously the thought of the forthcoming examination affects each student differently. Some lack confidence, some are over-confident; some will need encouragement while others will need to be a little more realistic in terms of their own ability.

Conclusion

Effective psychological preparation is very largely dependent on the quality of the analyses which are undertaken by the tutor or teacher following tests or examinations. Of themselves, the results of intermediate tests should not be regarded as being of critical importance, although the actual grades are the main concern of most students. What matters now is *how* the grade was achieved, and *how* a student can learn from the experience and be working to profit from it to improve his current performance. The overriding consideration is to build on successive test experiences with a view to the development of skill, ability, knowledge and the confidence to deal with the inherent stresses of competitive examinations.

References

Beard, R. M. and Sinclair, J. J. (1980) *Motivating Students.* Routledge and Kegan Paul, London.

Dansereau, D. F. et al. (1979) Cognitive approaches to learning strategies. In O'Neil, H. F. (Jr) and Spielberger, C. D. (eds). *Cognitive and Affective Learning Strategies.* Academic Press, New York.

Davies, D. E. (1985) Psychological approach to examinations. *Education and Training.* 27 (4), 127-8.

Desiderato, O. and Koshinen, P. (1969) Academic study habits and academic achievements. *Journal of Counselling Psychology.* 16, 162-5.

Gaa, J. P. (1971) The effects of individual goal setting conferences on achievement, attitudes and locus of control. Paper presented at the annual meeting of the American Educational Research Association, New York. February 1971.

Kearney, J. E. (1969) Success factors in tertiary education. *Australian Journal of Higher Education.* 3 (3), 231-7.

Maddox, H. (1963) *How to Study.* Pan Books, London.

Pentony, P. (1968) A study of students in academic difficulties. *Australian Journal of Higher Education.*

Poore, R. P. (Jr) and Pappas, J. P. (1974) A criterion related validity study of the McGraw-Hill Inventory of Study Habits and Attitudes. Paper presented at the annual meeting of the Rocky Mountain Psychological Association, Denver. May 1974.

Sarason, I. G. (1978). *Cognitive Interference Questionnaire.*

Tryon, G. S. (1980) The measurement and treatment of test anxiety. *Review of Education Research.* 50 (2), 343-72.

Wankowski, J. A. (1973). *Temperament, motivation and academic achievement.* University of Birmingham Educational Survey.

Wittmaier, B. C. (1972). Test anxiety and study habits. *Journal of Educational Research.* 65, 352-4.

Chapter 6

Maximizing Examination Performance

Introduction

Preparation for examinations, both in schools and in further and higher education, places almost total emphasis on the development of the intellectual capacities of individual students. However, despite much preparation, there are large numbers of students whose performance in competitive examinations continually fails to do justice to their ability, training and commitment, whose results appear to be almost incompatible with their talent and promise, and whose scripts are virtually unrecognizable from their course work assignments. In the author's survey, for example, 40 per cent of students reported that they generally did better in mock examinations than in the examination proper, and nearly 70 per cent felt that they could have done better at A level. Many students are simply overwhelmed by the cumulative effects of prolonged worry and chronic fatigue in the months before an examination and by the continued pressures operating in the examination situation. These pressures include, among others, the individually perceived importance of the examination, the presence of other candidates and invigilators, and, in many instances, the intimidating effect of large assembly halls. This contention is supported by the author's survey which showed that 13.3 per cent of A level students were 'worrying a lot' three months before the examination, and 32.3 per cent of students one month before. It is further supported by the finding that 60.5 per cent of students were troubled by various health problems arising from worry at this time. Under such stress there can be a retrogression in skilled performance concerning the writing of examination questions. Much of the advice concerning

119

examination technique is ignored, thus the questions are not attended to sufficiently, little or no planning takes place and, in many cases, students start writing almost straightaway.

Peak performance in academic examinations requires extensive preparation in the cognitive domain, the development of a constructive mood and approach, and efficient examination technique. Students also stand to gain to varying degrees from appropriate preparation in the affective domain. These areas of concern, although reviewed here separately, frequently interrelate. Thus high anxiety tends to be reflected in poor study habits and poor concentration; on the other hand, a confident attitude frequently means that the student has efficient study habits and good concentration.

Common weaknesses in examination scripts

Features of poor and inadequate examination scripts are outlined below:

1. An incorrect interpretation of the actual meaning of the question. Such a failing can of course arise for a number of reasons. These might include a poor understanding of the subject, a high level of test-anxiety, failure to study the question sufficiently and an inexact understanding of important terms which the question might contain. Maddox (1963) emphasizes the importance of students knowing the precise meaning of words which are frequently used in examination questions of the essay type. Maddox lists a number of keywords including 'discuss', 'evaluate', 'explain', 'review', 'interpret', 'contrast' and 'summarize'. The terms 'examine', 'assess' and 'determine' are also frequently used. Maddox suggests that in some cases students fail to identify the keyword in a question or, if they do, may be uncertain of its exact meaning. Clearly it is of vital importance that the student checks that he knows the precise meaning of keywords commonly employed in questions of the essay type.

2. Scripts which are confused, disorganized, fragmented and which show little evidence of planning; as a result they lack coherency and clarity.

3. Scripts containing global, general answers to questions calling for a specific, direct response.

4. Scripts with responses which simply are not in answer to the questions posed. For example, an oblique response is given which appears to be a prepared or set answer to a different question than the one posed. Thus although the student, in this case, may have some knowledge and understanding of the material this must be limited as is evident from the inflexibility of the response. Such answers to 'expected' questions are not uncommon.

Characteristics of good scripts

Examiners will be favourably influenced by answers having the following characteristics:

1. Clarity of discussion. This is of the essence, as answers need to be factual, concise and explicit.
2. Well-balanced argument supported by brief references to relevant source materials in terms of authors, books, articles, research investigations and television and radio documentaries. It is the *evidence* which is important. If an accurate reference is known the precise details can be given in a footnote. This of course adds considerable weight to anything the student might have to say. Balance means that the main aspects of the question receive due consideration from the writer and that one particular aspect is not unduly overemphasized to the relative neglect of others.
3. Well-organized, coherent responses directed towards meeting the specific demands of the question.
4. A meaningful grasp of the particular problem or issue and a sound overall knowledge of the general subject area. This can be shown in several ways which are outlined in the following section on examination technique.

Examination technique

There are a number of elementary, perhaps rather obvious but none the less important, procedures which students must remember to follow. First, the instructions on the question paper need to be studied very carefully. Instructions contain important information for the student including the duration of the examination, the number of questions to be answered,

121

the choices and alternatives available and, in some cases, the marks allocated for each question. Second, the paper should be carefully read through and a note made of the questions which initially appeal. Third, a question should be selected which the student likes and to which he feels he can give an adequate answer. Fourth, a plan or outline answer should be drawn up. In a two and a half- or three-hour paper some ten minutes should be allocated for this preliminary work. Finally, and with regular reference to the outline or framework, the writing of the full answer can be undertaken.

The above procedures need to be practised as part of a student's preparation programme. Time needs to be given over to developing a well-rehearsed, well-established routine to be followed at the commencement of an examination. Practising the above procedures and working to the strict time-scale of ten minutes for a two and a half- or three-hour paper will mean that a candidate can quickly adapt to the actual examination situation. A virtually automatic routine means that uncertainty is reduced, anxiety accordingly lowered and concentration enhanced.

Most papers of the essay type have a choice of questions. Time needs, therefore, to be spent in learning to review questions. The aim here is to learn to appreciate what the examiner is asking and to identify the salient features of the question with increasing speed and efficiency. This will help the student to arrive at accurate, firm decisions concerning which questions are to be answered. In arriving at quick, accurate decisions with respect to question selection, the checklist which appears on page 113 could also be used.

Planning answers

In the first place it is imperative that the student makes quite sure that he has a clear understanding of the meaning of the question. Then the question needs to be very carefully studied and the student must be quite certain in his own mind what it is that the examiner is asking before he starts to write. Planning answers will help to ensure that the criteria of a competent, creditable answer can be met as fully as possible.

Planning answers to examination questions improves with practice. The aim of planning is to develop a relevant, logical, coherent, well-organized and factual response to the question posed. At the same time the candidate needs to take every opportunity to demonstrate to the examiner that he has a sound grasp of the problem. Ways in which this can be done are discussed later in this section.

In reviewing a question the aim is to learn to identify the salient features or major points with increasing speed and efficiency and then to formulate an outline answer. It is useful to jot down points as they occur — the major ones can then be listed in order, together with supporting material in the form of references, examples, comparisons, illustrations and exceptions. An outline or framework to which the student can refer from time to time, as he writes, is needed. This will help to ensure that the material being used is relevant. Points which occur to the writer later on can be added as footnotes rather than attempting to rewrite whole passages.

As we have shown, it is important to plan answers. However, despite numerous reminders to the effect, it seems to be the case that many students start writing almost straightaway, that attempts at planning answers, therefore, are largely discarded and the advice to do so is ignored. In test situations some students have reported experiencing feelings of being rushed when working alongside others and, at the extreme being close to panic. The following are typical of the comments which some students make:

- 'Everyone else seemed to be writing.'
- 'I felt I had to write as much as I could.'
- 'I just felt I had to start.'
- 'I felt I couldn't afford the time to make plans.'
- 'I felt in such a hurry.'

In fact it can be generally assumed that planning answers saves both time and effort; it indicates to the student whether he has sufficient material to answer the question fully. It will help to reduce the risk of a student embarking on an answer only to find that he does not really understand the question or has insufficient material at his command. In this way he is less likely to be switching 'to and fro' from one question to another. Table 6 on the behaviour of A level examination candidates shows the findings of the author's survey.

Table 6 *Panic reactions of A level students*

Student behaviour	%
Switching to and fro from one question to another	35.9
Continual checking and rechecking of work	25.3
Dizziness and fainting	4.2

Adequate planning would help to eliminate unproductive and stress-provoking activity. Planning means that there is less likelihood of unnecessary repetition and the use of irrelevant material which subsequently has to be discarded. Without sufficient planning the student is often forced to revise and even rewrite whole sections of his answer as points occur to him that alter his appreciation of, and therefore his approach to, the problem. Thus the student who engages in planning is in a much better position to write at speed and to the point, and there is far less risk of his becoming lost and confused than if he had begun his answer without a skeleton outline of the main areas and issues with their supporting examples and illustrations.

Without careful planning there exists the very real risk of answers being rambling and incoherent. Planning means that the student is in a much better position to present a balanced, coherent and meaningful response to the question. Lack of planning is one of the main reasons why, in many cases, examination scripts can be almost unrecognizable from the standards which students typically achieve in their course work.

In preparing for examinations which consist of questions of the essay type it is sound practice to set aside an hour twice a week right from the beginning of the course to review a paper, select a question, plan an outline and then finally write the answer. Regular practice of this kind will be reflected in improved results. Effective habits will be developed which will help to reduce the effects of stress. Furthermore, where a student answers a number of questions on the same topic, this provides him with the opportunity to view the topic from various perspectives and leads to greater understanding. By keeping to a strict timetable the whole process of tackling the paper is speeded up. The editorial staff of national newspapers are frequently required to present a critical report of a major news item in a matter of hours. This means analysing the problem, sifting the evidence and presenting a convincing, well-supported argument to a critical readership; the pressures can be immense with whole careers and reputations at stake. The newspaper editor is an example of how repeated daily practice results in skilled performance.

It is a good idea to undertake some of this practice in the company of a few other students. In this way an individual can learn to deal with distractions and to concentrate on the question — in effect he starts learning to accommodate himself to the pressures of working alongside other people.

In answering questions of the essay-type a good intro-duction is important. In the opening paragraphs the student should aim to demonstrate that he has a sound appreciation of the salient issues raised by the question so that it is quickly apparent to the examiner that he is familiar with his material. Introductions tend to be overlong and peripheral. Thus, it is often a promising strategy to go straight to the core of the question and then to elaborate and qualify particular points in developing the answer.

An example of a convincing opening paragraph in answer to a question set for BEd students in physical education some years ago is given below:

Q: 'Practice is a necessary but not a sufficient condition for the mastery of skills. Discuss.'

A: 'Since skills are learned then clearly practice must be a necessary condition for learning to take place. However, other factors are important and often necessary for the acquisition of skills. These include appropriate guidance and instruction, motivation, knowledge of results and factors which vary with the learner including age, ability, intelligence, strength and previous experience. One investigation, for example, concluded that knowledge of results is the strongest, most important variable controlling learning (Bilodeau and Bilodeau, 1961). Again, if the individual is not motivated to learn then little improvement will occur and any practice becomes a waste of time. Sheer repetition, therefore, does not necessarily result in any improvement in the skilled performance of an activity. Indeed, some practice can be harmful and inhibit progress towards the mastery of skills, Faulty techniques, for example, acquired during unsupervised practice will have to be unlearned if progress towards the mastery of skills is to be facilitated.'

The above opening paragraph meets the criteria for a com-petent opening response to the question. It is clear, relevant, concise and quickly conveys to the reader that the writer has a sound grasp of the central issues concerning the subject. Research evidence is cited and an accurate reference given which adds considerable weight to the argument.

A second example (also taken from a BEd in physical education paper) of an opening which meets the criteria of clarity, succinctness, relevance, analysis and thus competence follows:

Q: 'Estimate the value of competition in acquiring sports skills.'

A: 'Competition can be an incentive and is a useful motivational technique provided it is used wisely and is closely related to the needs of the athlete. Temperament, emotional maturity, ability, past experiences of success or failure and coach/athlete relationships are important factors to take into account in the planning of competitive learning situations. Moderate competition between individuals provides interest and enjoyment. However, there are dangers implicit in competitive situations. Knapp (1963) points to the risk of antagonisms arising between both individuals and groups. She also considers that competition may impede progress when athletes concentrate upon winning at a particular level and neglect to develop the skills to perform successfully at higher levels. Competitive situations can generate high levels of stress and can lead to negative attitudes, anxiety and a lowering of motivation. Learning situations in which individuals are being continually outclassed or which regularly pose a serious threat to prestige and self-esteem should be avoided. The Lawn Tennis Association's emphasis on continual competitive play, for example, results in many promising players opting out of the game by the age of 16 for less harrowing pursuits (Davies, 1981).

The value of competition is considerable in situations in which an individual can compete against himself in the sense that he competes against his own previous standard. Competition against the self presents a meaningful challenge and avoids social antagonisms. A student can also compete against other recognized, established standards of performance which pertain in athletics and swimming, for example. Objective knowledge of results is highly motivating and provides an incentive to strive for higher standards of performance.'

In this second example it soon becomes evident that the writer is thoroughly conversant with the salient issues which are raised by the question.

Cognitive preparation

As we emphasized in Chapter 5, frequent testing of material has several advantages and is seen as a central feature of a cognitive preparation programme. A further effective method which is not generally employed in any systematic way is to spend some time in actually teaching the subject or material Teaching requires the ability to explain and thus gives rise to greater understanding. In explaining a topic or problem there is often the need to illustrate, compare, contrast, synthesize and analyse; it also frequently becomes necessary to view issues and problems from different perspectives. Teachers often report that following a year's teaching they know far more about their subject than they did when they completed their professional examinations. Similarly, students find that the giving of seminars generally provides them with a much better grasp of issues and problems than does the writing of essays. Thus, it is good practice for a small group of students to get together and take turns in teaching topics to others. Alternatively, if this is not possible, a student could teach an imaginary class.

Concentration

A number of studies (Deffenbecher et al. 1979) indicate that the ability of high-anxious people to concentrate upon a set task is relatively poor. This seems to be particularly the case when working in conditions of considerable stress. What appears to happen is that the more stressful the situation the more time anxious people spend worrying. Deffenbacker's research, for example, showed that in conditions of high stress anxious students spent 60 per cent of their time actually engaged in the task, but that the amount rose to 80 per cent in conditions of low stress.

Poor concentration stems from two main sources. These are a negative attitude or mood, and the ease with which students are distracted from a set task. Anxious students tend to become worried about their own poor performance and about how much better the others are. They also worry about past failures, letting people down and having no luck. The negative attitude of high-anxious people is underlined by their tendency to ascribe failure to their lack of ability. In contrast, people of a more stable disposition tend to believe that failure, in their case, can be put down to lack of effort. Thus, following failure comparatively stable individuals tend to respond with increased effort while the response of anxious people is to spend even more time in worrying about their lack of ability.

The problem for high-anxious students is that when they are faced with a test of their ability they tend to become overwhelmed by a variety of negative emotions and feelings which can include anger, fear, guilt and remorse. Frequently, these negative emotions are accompanied by negative self-talk and images which serve seriously to disrupt concentration on the task in hand.

The control of concentration

The first step in the development of the management of concentration is a diagnosis which will reveal detailed information for both teacher and student concerning the nature of the problem. Students need to experience situations which will help them to become aware of their attentional difficulties in terms of why and how they become distracted from the task in hand. With an awareness of the nature, source and length of the distraction periods, specific, individualized treatment programmes can be designed.

The work of Professor Robert M. Niddefer (1976), although concerned with sports performance, has obvious implications for academic situations in which performance is being evaluated. The Test of Attention and Interpersonal Style (TAIS) measures a number of attentional styles and the author seeks to relate particular styles to expected differences in performance. Poor concentration, it is argued, arises from both external and internal overload. A student with a high external overload is distracted by irrelevant stimuli, such as the presence of other people, noise and unfamiliar surroundings. With a high internal overload concentration is lowered by the student's own internal thoughts; he may be thinking about the social consequences of failure and be overconcerned about the prospect of loss of prestige and status. Some students literally become trapped by their own thoughts and feelings and their performance is inhibited thereby. Students with high overloads have difficulty in analysing problems and fail to comprehend what is required of them. Niddefer considers that people with overload attentional styles tend to perform badly under pressure and to be anxious people generally. Training in relaxation and meditation is recommended if the attentional style of the anxious student is to be more effective and thus enhance performance.

Fatigue

Loss of concentration can be a feature of any prolonged period of intensive study culminating in an examination which may cover a period of several days or even weeks. With increasing mental and physical fatigue concentration starts to deteriorate with the student ceasing to be sufficiently involved mentally in the answers to questions. Concentration can be adversely affected by the physical discomfort arising from tense and tired muscles. Fatigue effects become greater as the mental demands on an individual increase. Thus the well-prepared, well-organized student will be less vulnerable to fatigue effects than the unprepared one because the task of dealing with the paper is less difficult. Furthermore, the well-prepared student, who is thoroughly conversant with examination technique, has a well-rehearsed routine concerning the procedures to be followed and can proceed smoothly through the paper without being involved in a lot of self-correcting, checking and re-checking of his work. He has, in effect, less to do because he has done it all so many times before.

The onset of fatigue may also be accompanied by feelings of anxiety and insecurity, with a student beginning to experience misgivings about the adequacy of his performance. This, in turn, leads to a further deterioration in performance since concentration is again adversely affected. With fatigue, it becomes more difficult to sustain concentration, to make decisions and to organize material. Fatigue effects tend to be greater for new situations than for familiar ones. Stress and, therefore, fatigue, are likely to be greater when working in a large, strange assembly hall than in a familiar classroom or study, for example.

The ability to concentrate completely on the paper is a critical factor in examination performance. The test of a person's ability to concentrate is determined by the extent to which he is able to shut out from conscious awareness the various stimuli which are irrelevant and distracting. So, noisy interferences, behaviour of other examinees, movements of the invigilator, temperature of the room and thoughts of possible outcomes must all be ignored. In this way all the student's mental energy is concentrated on the question being answered which is the correct situation.

The ability to concentrate in the examination situation is a skill which has to be learned by practice; it is little use for a candidate to just remind himself to 'concentrate' during the examination. He can employ cue words to remind himself to concentrate, but the value of these will stem from his experience of simulated examination conditions and from the extensive mental practice which has been undertaken beforehand, in which he has worked through examination papers visualizing himself concentrating on a particular question.

Time needs to be spent in cultivating a positive attitude towards examinations. A number of support strategies used either in isolation or in various combinations are available to help the student to do this.

Cognitive modification, as described in Chapter 3, is an important strategy in the case of students who are unreasonably pessimistic and who approach examinations with negative attitudes.

Lack of confidence and negative self-critical thoughts which interfere with concentration can be countered by using relaxation during the actual examination in combination with positive self-talk and images. Spielberger et al. (1979) report that a significant improvement in grades was found for students who used relaxation and anxiety-coping techniques. These techniques, Spielberger considers, appear to lead to increased confidence by reducing negative self-criticism and through the control of uncomfortable distractions, emotional feelings and reactions. Work by Dansereau (1979) showed that self-initiated relaxation used in combination with positive self-talk or self-coaching facilitated performance both under non-distracting conditions and under distracting conditions (noise). With relaxation, the aim is to practise until this state of lowered arousal can be achieved in a matter of seconds following, for example, a deep breath, a click of the fingers or a cue word. Relaxation thus becomes a cue-controlled technique. The aim is for the skill of relaxation to be increasingly employed in everyday situations and finally in competitively stressful situations such as examinations. With self-talk or self-coaching, students, in the style of an athletic coach, aim to talk themselves into a positive, constructive mood and approach towards test-evaluative situations. In Dansereau's work students were taught to monitor their moods and to counter distractions by the use of positive self-talk and relaxation. The use of positive statements helps to direct attention towards the task in hand.

The author has suggested to students that they could be using statements such as the following in their psychological preparation:

> 'Now I know how to relax I shall do much better.'
> 'I am going to pass that examination.'
> 'My attitude is changing for the better.'
> 'I shall be concentrating on the question and nothing else.'
> 'I feel calm.'

The use of autogenic phrases and cue words is a technique which has also been found to improve concentration (Wenz and Story, 1977; Ziegler, 1978).

Mental practice or mental rehearsal

A technique which can be used to develop confidence and improve concentration is that of mental practice or mental rehearsal. There are strong claims for the use of this technique in terms of improved performance (Suinn, 1977). With this method the individual can visualize or picture himself sitting the examination in a calm, purposeful manner, his whole attention being focused on the question paper. He is not a spectator in the exercise but is actively involved, in a mental sense, in sitting the examination in this particular way. The idea is to get as vivid an image as possible of working in a controlled, assured manner. The technique needs to be actively and repeatedy practised until the particular mental pictures can be summoned at will. During this mental rehearsal the student should keep positive goals in mind. He should picture and imagine positive outcomes such as completing a satisfactory answer to a question. The technique involves thinking, visualizing and finally coming to believe in positive outcomes. Mental rehearsal sessions should be preceded by relaxation exercises so that the individual is totally relaxed before engaging in the activity. Mental rehearsal or visualization is used frequently by athletes competing at international level and can be as effective, if not more so, as actual physical practice of an activity or skill. The technique is also employed in the cultivation of a constructive mood and approach towards competitive test situations. Furthermore, positive mental imagery can be employed to sustain concentration. The student can visualize himself being relaxed and concentrating entirely on the question.

A most effective way of developing a positive attitude and a constructive approach towards examinations is through the completion of successful learning experiences. A series of good performances in short tests completed under examination conditions, will help considerably in most cases. Although the student is given a choice the tests need require that only one question be answered. The ability to work and study persistently is also very strongly influenced by experiences of this kind (Sears, 1940). Good and Brophy (1973) emphasize that students will generally lose interest if they do not achieve some success. The quality of persistence is also important in an examination or test context; some students, for example, give up far too early in the face of initial difficulty. In retrospect they concede that had they persisted with the paper they could have done considerably better.

The above techniques and strategies can, of course, be employed in other situations which the student perceives as stressful. These might include sports competitions, interviews, speaking at debates, giving a seminar or teaching a lesson, for example. In such situations, positive feedback from the use of these stress reduction measures provides the student with evidence that the measures are effective, that they serve to reduce stress and thus enhance performance. There is likely therefore, to be a beneficial spin-off effect with respect to sitting examinations since the student can view these strategies and techniques as tried and tested measures which he now knows are working for him. Such experiences will give the student a better idea of how to cope with stress and he will thus have considerably more control over the test situation than formerly. He should feel more secure generally and accordingly have more confidence in his ability to succeed.

Gaining success in particular activities is likely to be effective in changing an individual's self-perception from someone who fails to someone who can succeed. A person with a history of failure concerning examinations, or any test of performance under pressure, may well have formed negative concepts concerning his ability to the extent that he will almost be expecting to do badly. Success needs to be achieved in a test or competition as this will serve to raise his confidence and change his attitude for the better.

At all age levels students who have the support of an understanding, knowledgeable advisor will find this a great help in preparing themselves psychologically for examinations. The advisor who can nurture a student's interest in a subject is invaluable in helping to cope with the frustrations and stresses of long-term study. An empathic advisor who is constructive, can foster self-esteem and can encourage a student to have pride in his achievements, will greatly assist that student to react positively in test situations. What is required is an ongoing objective analysis of a student's performance in preliminary tests and the ability to interpret unsuccessful outcomes in a positive way.

References

Bilodeau, E. A., and Bilodeau, I. McD. (1961) Motor skills learning. *The Annual Review of Psychology* 12, 243-80.

Dansereau, D. F. et al. (1979) Cognitive approaches to learning strategies. In O'Neil, H. F. (Jr) and Spielberger, C. D. (eds) Cognitive and Affective Learning Strategies. Academic Press, New York.

Davies, D. E. (1981) Psychological and social psychological factors in the training of potential tennis champions. *Medisport.* 3 (4), 110-15.

Davies, D. E. (1986) *Examination Performance: a survey of the stress-related problems of A level students.* Unpublished survey.

Deffenbecher, J. L., Mathis, H. and Michaels, A. C. (1979) Two self-control procedures in the reduction of targeted and non-targeted anxieties. *Journal of Counselling Psychology.* 26, 120-27.

Good, T. L. and Brophy, J. E. (1973) Looking in Classrooms. Harper and Row, New York.

Knapp, B. (1963) *Skill in Sport.* Routledge and Kegan Paul, London.

Maddox, H. (1963) *How to Study.* Pan Books, London.

Niddefer, R. M. (1976) Test of attentional and interpersonal style. *Journal of Personality and Social Psychology.* 34, 394-404.

Spielberger, C. D. et al. (1979) Test anxiety reduction, learning strategies and academic performance. In O'Neil, H. F. (Jr) and Spielberger, C. D. (eds) *Cognitive and Affective Learning Strategies.* Academic Press, New York.

Sears, P. (1940) Level of aspiration in academically successful and unsuccessful children. *Journal of Abnormal and Social Psychology.* 35, 498-536.

Suinn, R. M. (1980) *Psychology in Sports.* Burgess, Minneapolis.

Wenz, B. J. and Story, D. (1977) *An application of Biofeedback and Relaxation Procedures with a Group of Superior Athletes.* Unpublished manuscript.

Ziegler, S. (1978) An overview of anxiety management strategies in sport. In Straub, W. F. *Sport Psychology.* Mouvement Publications, New York.

Chapter 7

Confidence: A Popular Viewpoint

Loss of confidence

The ease with which confidence can be lost was dramatically illustrated in a study concerning the effects on self-esteem of favourable and unfavourable performance reports (Ross, L. et al., 1975). Subjects were arbitrarily divided into two groups and then each group performed the same problem-solving task. On completing the task one group was told that they had done badly and the other group that they had done very well. In actual fact no grading had been made and the subjects were given false information. Some time was allowed for this information to 'sink in' before the subjects were told the truth — that their performance had not been scored at all. The subjects were then asked to give a subjective assessment of their own ability concerning their performance and to estimate their scores. They were also asked to make estimates concerning their future performances. The 'failure' group gave markedly lower estimates with respect to both their current performance and their expected future performance than did the 'successful' group. The results of this piece of research demonstrate how vulnerable some people are to the negative effects of exposure to failure situations and underline the extent to which an individual's expectations of success or failure can be influenced by the ratings of others. Estimates of future performance still continue to be influenced by the initial ratings of others even when these are known to have been false.

Developing confidence: some general strategies

Confidence is, in effect, a firm belief in one's own abilities. It is essentially an assured expectation of being successful.

In the development of confidence a preparation programme must be designed which will bring a lot of success. This is particularly important in the case of the test-anxious student because, as has been stressed earlier, failure experiences should be avoided as they lead to increased worry and, therefore, adversely affect both concentration and aspiration levels. The programme would consist of a series of test questions and papers that must be completed successfully. In order to ensure that the student experiences a lot of success a number of important steps and guidelines need to be followed. First, the student should become thoroughly conversant with good examination technique. This means practice in decision making, in reviewing and understanding questions, and in drafting outline answers. Second, the student must acquire efficient study habits. Third, the test-anxious student must acquire the relaxation technique to the extent that he can employ this skill in conditions which are perceived as stressful, such as performing in the presence of others. Fourth, the student should have a thorough knowledge of the subject or the sections of it to be tested. Students generally lose interest if they do not meet, at least periodically, with some success. It is important, therefore, that assignments and test questions are closely related to the ability and experience of the student, particularly in the case of the test-anxious student who tends to falter and worry in the face of challenge in test-evaluative situations. Failure experiences must be avoided. A programme of tests and test questions needs to be very carefully graded and learning thoroughly consolidated before more difficult items are tackled. With a thorough knowledge of the subject, the adverse effects of examination stress will accordingly be minimized. The areas of the syllabus which will be vulnerable under stress are those which have been insufficiently learned.

A preparation programme and suggested guidelines

The programme outlined below is designed to help students generally, but in particular to help those who find examinations to be both a stressful and worrying experience, and those who may be working largely on their own. The programme represents a wider, more systematic approach towards tackling examinations than those which students traditionally follow. It is a psychological programme of preparation. Psychological preparation is seen as incorporating a sustained, systematic approach to an attainable standard of performance. Students should aim to become increasingly psychologically tough or resilient, and at the same time to cultivate a positive, assertive approach to the examination situation. The programme includes a number of learning strategies and techniques which are seen to be basic to the academic and emotional needs of anxious students. It aims to maximize examination performance through increased confidence, sustained concentration and efficient technique.

The programme is grouped into two major areas of concern for the student. The first of these is devoted to the management of concentration and to certain stress reduction techniques for coping with anxiety and worry. The second area is concerned with the academic or technical aspects of preparation and performance. For an appreciation of why particular strategies and techniques are being recommended, reference should be made to the appropriate chapters in the text as indicated. In particular the section which deals with the management of stress in Chapter 3 should be consulted. The programme can be complemented by the employment of additional stress reduction techniques described in the text which individual students may find suitable for their needs. Anxious students, for example, find 'modelling behaviour' to be particularly helpful.

1. The management of concentration: relaxation, positive self-talk and self-coaching

(i) Learn to relax. Practise progressive relaxation daily. The programme contained in Chapter 3 takes about 20 minutes. After 12 weeks the programme can be speeded up considerably and the time reduced to five minutes. Self-induced relaxation (SIR) is an integral part of the preparation programme. SIR can be practised, incidentally, at odd times during the day, such as when waiting in queues or travelling on buses and trains. Practise the exercises every day and note the gradual improvement in your ability to reduce tension as you progress towards the stage where you are a much more relaxed person generally. After a few months of daily practice a deep breath, a click of the fingers or a cue word can be used to induce relaxation. In time, as a result of extensive daily practice you will reach the stage when you will be able to relax in a matter of seconds. Relaxation can also be used during the actual examination and will help to inhibit any panic reactions, such as indecision, which may arise.

If you wish to have objective confirmation of your progress towards acquiring the relaxation response you can do this by following a simple biofeedback procedure of measuring fingertip temperature (Chapter 3). In the more relaxed state this will be higher than normal because the flow of blood to the extremities of the body will be facilitated.

(ii) Develop a constructive mood and a positive approach towards tests and examinations. There are several ways in which this can be done. Use positive statements and repeat these over and over again until they are said almost involuntarily. You can make up your own statements but an example of a positive statement would be, 'I shall be going out to do my very best'. Positive statements serve to direct a student's attention to the task before him and to improve concentration. Repeated use of positive statements will encourage a student to start thinking positively and to acquire positive concepts. Eliminate all self-critical, deprecative self-comments.

A positive approach and constructive mood can also be cultivated by keeping in mind images and experiences of successful past performances concerning course assignments and tests, for example.

(iii) Endeavour to become intrinsically motivated to study your subject. In this way your attention will be focused on acquiring knowledge and developing ability. Social considerations are more likely to assume secondary importance and the attendant stresses will be correspondingly less. You should become less worried about letting people down and about what others might think, for example. Setting clearly-defined, weekly goals can help to facilitate intrinsic motivation.

2. Academic preparation and examination technique
(i) Acquire effective study habits and follow a regular programme of study. Writers such as Maddox emphasize the importance of personal organization and the need to learn methods of study. Set weekly goals that are clear and

realistic, and write these down or announce them publicly. Test your ability to achieve these goals. Testing provides you with knowledge of your progress and acts as a powerful incentive to continue to study (Chapter 5).

(ii) Teach a topic related to a particular question to a small group of fellow students each week. Alternatively, teach the topic to an imaginary audience. Spend, for example, 30 minutes on exposition followed by around 15 minutes on discussion or, alternatively, self-evaluation.

Teaching requires you to explain and often to view a topic from several perspectives. In this way you gain insights, a greater appreciation of the salient issues and, consequently, a sound knowledge of the subject.

(iii) The more skilled you become at answering essay questions, the less likelihood there is of your performance breaking down under competitive stress. Furthermore, mastery of this skill reduces anxiety because the task of writing essays is now perceived as being less difficult. Right from the start of your course, therefore, it is recommended that you practise as follows:

— write two answers to examination questions of the essay-type each week on separate occasions;
— get as near as you can to the real conditions of the examination;
— stick rigidly to the actual procedures, in particular, the time limit;
— get a friend or relative to act as invigilator;
— ask a teacher or fellow student to evaluate your answer or, failing this, carry out your own evaluation.

In this way examinations will begin to lose some of their strangeness and, therefore, their stress. In the case of a three-hour paper consisting of five questions, set aside ten minutes to study the instructions, review the paper as a whole and select a question. This leaves just 34 minutes for each question. Thus, if you are answering two questions, 20 minutes' reading time, 68 minutes on the questions and 42 minutes to evaluate both answers, gives a total time of two hours and ten minutes per week.

Reading time, paper 1, question 1	10 minutes
Completion of question 1	34 minutes
Evaluation of question 1	21 minutes
Reading time, paper 2, question 2	10 minutes
Completion of question 2	34 minutes
Evaluation of question 2	21 minutes
	130 minutes
	or 2 hours and 10 minutes

Essay questions can be used as a means of testing the extent to which weekly goals have been achieved.

(iv) The time immediately before and at the beginning of an examination is when stress and tension are at their highest levels. So, get lots of test papers and keep practising how you will begin until you have such a well-established routine that it becomes virtually automatic. In this way you are less likely to become overanxious when it comes to the actual examination. There is no need to work right through the paper, just practise the following procedure, imagining that this is the examination proper: look at the paper; study the instructions; read through the set questions and select a question; draft an outline answer. Allow ten minutes for preliminary reading of the paper and about seven minutes for planning the outline. This procedure can be practised twice a week and will help you to adapt quickly to examination conditions.

Health

During this preparation period it is important to keep in good health. A healthy person is in a much better condition to tolerate long periods of study and is less vulnerable to stress and fatigue. It is generally felt that regular daily exercise is beneficial both physiologically and psychologically because it provides a means of releasing excessive muscle tension. It is widely considered that exercise leads to improved sleep and consequently increased energy. With respect to sleep it is important to keep to regular times for going to bed and getting up. For good health, attention should also be paid to following a proper diet; this is also important for combating stress and fatigue.

140

Summary

Examination stress can be managed. One suggested programme of preparation has been outlined. It includes strategies and techniques which are known to be effective in minimizing the disruptive effects of stress and worry. Practices have been described for the management of concentration, for the development of a positive approach, and for effective performance in stressful competitive situations. The needs of individual students vary but for students who find examinations a stressful and worrying experience regular, sustained practice over an extended period of time is recommended for improved concentration and thus for the enhancement of performance.

References

Maddox, H. (1963) *How to Study*. Pan Books, London.

Ross, L., Lepper, M. R. and Hubbard, M. (1975) Perseverance in
self-perception and social perception: biased attributional processes
in the debriefing paradigm. *Journal of Personality and Social
Psychology*. 32, 880-92.

Index